Grand Marais, MN 55604

OUR CHURCH

Gordon G. Johnson
adapted by Bob Putman

The contents of this book have been adapted from **My Church** by Gordon G. Johnson, published by Harvest Publications.

HARVEST PUBLICATIONS
Arlington Heights, Illinois

Second printing 1987

© *1984 by Harvest Publications*
Library of Congress Card Catalog Number 83-82990
Printed in the United States of America

All rights are reserved. No part of this book may be reproduced in any manner whatsoever without written permission from the publisher, except in the case of brief quotations embodied in critical articles and reviews.

Unless otherwise identified, Scripture quotations are taken from The Holy Bible: New International Version, *copyright* © *1978 by The New York International Bible Society, used by permission of Zondervan Bible Publishers. Other versions used are* The New Testament in Modern English, *Rev. Edn. J.B. Phillips, translator,* © *J. Phillips 1958, 1960, 1972; and* The Living Bible *(verses marked TLB), copyright 1971 by Tyndale House Publishers, Wheaton, IL. Used by permission.*

Published by Harvest Publications
Division of the Board of Educational Ministries
Baptist General Conference
2002 S. Arlington Heights Road
Arlington Heights, IL 60005

ISBN: *0-935797-06-8*

CONTENTS

1. Church Built on a Book 5
   (God's Word)
2. More Than a Building 17
   (Jesus Christ)
3. A Very Important Idea 27
   (access to God)
4. Showing You Believe 37
   (membership)
5. Showing You Belong 49
   (baptism)
6. When Remembering Is Worship 57
   (Lord's Supper)
7. Keeping Things in Order 65
   (organization)
8. A Secret You Can't Keep 75
   (witness and mission)
9. Taking Care of Borrowed Stuff 85
   (stewardship)
10. You've Got Connections 97
    (fellowship)
11. Worship: Our Response to a Holy God 109
    (worship)
12. God + Ideas + People = History 121
    (our heritage)
13. Similar, Yet Different 135
    (Baptist distinctives)

Dictionary 143

1 Church Built on a Book

Eddie stopped his bicycle to watch the cement truck. It lumbered over the curb and began to lug backwards toward an open hole, which was lined with wooden forms. A carpenter signaled directions from beside the truck as it lurched backwards over the broken ground.

When it reached the hole, the carpenter waved and the truck stopped suddenly. The driver climbed out and shifted a few levers. The motor began to make a low, grinding sound. Eddie watched as chunky, wet concrete slid down into the hole. It gurgled into the wooden forms, where the builders busily shaped and smoothed it.

When the forms were filled, the driver pulled the truck forward and rinsed off the cement. Then he climbed back into the cab and drove away, back wheels lurching over the curb. Eddie wondered what the cement was for. After a few minutes he jumped his bike over the curb and rode home.

Eddie stopped at the construction site several times in the next few days. The carpenters were busy building a house on the cement they had poured and shaped. He realized that the cement made a solid, strong base for the house.

Eddie had watched the carpenters building a foundation. Every building needs a foundation so that it will be strong. The church also needs a strong foundation. It needs a leader and guidelines for its meeting, worship, fellowship and method of sharing its faith in Jesus Christ with the community and the world.

In our day there are many groups of people that speak of themselves as a church of Jesus Christ. Each of these groups depends on one or more materials to build its foundation. A church may build its life on tradition, on what seems right (but may not be), or on the Bible. All are important, but we believe the Bible is most important. The

Bible helps us make decisions. It is our authority.

Tradition is Not a Good Base

What is tradition? That's a good question. Any custom or practice that you have been doing for a long time is a tradition. Some people say that they celebrate Easter, Thanksgiving, or Christmas by doing the same things in the same way each year because, "We've always done it that way." Their celebrations have become traditions.

The people that make up a church may think that because something has always been done they should keep doing the same thing. Sometimes they do this even though their beliefs and actions may not agree with the Bible. Of course, all churches believe that some of the decisions made by church leaders in the past are still good today. And many are. But when these decisions contradict the clear teaching of the Bible, they are built on a foundation that will break down.

Christians are under the authority of the Bible. Church history and tradition are important, but the Bible is the main authority for the way Christians live and for what they believe. It is the main way God talks to us about who He is, what He does and how we relate to Him.

Our Own Ideas Are Not a Good Base

Every day you have to make decisions. Will I do my homework or watch TV? How should I spend my allowance? Should I do what my friends are doing even if I think they're wrong? You probably make many decisions based upon your own sense of what is right. But sometimes what seems to be the right way to do something is not God's way of doing it. That is because God's wisdom is much greater than ours.

Many times in the history of the church, people have had to make decisions based on their own ideas. Sometimes this has been very good. Other times they may have done things which the Bible says are wrong.

Our ideas are constantly changing. Because they are, decisions in the church would change as often as someone has a new idea. God's Word is true and never changes. It is a reliable source of instruction for us to follow. So we use the Bible as our guide.

The guiding rule in the churches of the Baptist General Conference is to obey and live by the teaching of the Bible. We think the New Testament is most useful, since it was written for the people who make up the church. We should not do anything in our lives or in the church that opposes what is taught in the New Testament.

THE BIBLE IS THE MAIN AUTHORITY FOR WHAT CHRISTIANS BELIEVE AND HOW THEY SHOULD LIVE.

The Bible Is the True Base

What would have happened if the cement truck in the beginning of this chapter had been filled with mud rather than concrete? The foundation would have dried up and cracked, probably crumbling the moment someone tried to build on it. Several of the laborers would have gotten mad at each other and the house would not have been finished on time.

Like buildings, the church must have a solid, strong foundation. Your church believes that the Bible gives that kind of foundation and it is the only authority for our faith and actions. All churches in the Baptist General Conference have this belief. When we say that the Bible is our authority, we mean both the Old and New Testaments. But we emphasize the New Testament. It is the New Testament that tells us plainly about the life, death and resurrection of Jesus Christ, God's Son, and how His death for us can change the life of every person. It also tells us how the first Christian churches began and some of the future events in world history.

The Bible is One of a Kind

The Bible has several qualities which no other writings on earth can claim. First, it has *complete teaching for all spiritual purposes.* The words of the Bible are true—always. How can that be possible? Every word in the Bible was inspired by God and written by His servants. By inspired we mean that God breathed His truth into the minds of men, who wrote down what He told them. "For prophecy never had its origin in the will of man, but men spoke from God as they were carried along by the Holy Spirit" (2 Peter 1:21). Moses, David, Paul and many others wrote down God's truth as they saw it in human history or heard it directly from God. God Himself kept them from making mistakes.

The Bible tells us about God's creative works and about His relationship with the nation Israel. It also speaks about Christ (in both the Old and New Testaments) and about the beginning and function of the church. Because the author of the Bible is God, it is the perfect guide for the church. He never makes mistakes or does anything poorly. The

Bible is complete in itself.

Second, the Bible is *reliable*. It never changes. Many years ago men didn't believe that our continent exists; they thought the world was flat. Christopher Columbus disproved that idea when he discovered North America. As a result, scientists had to change their ideas about the shape of the world and its place in the universe.

Whether in science or in the church, men's ideas are always subject to change. But the Bible abides, it is certain, unchangeable. We may learn more truth from it or see its truth in a different way, but the Bible is itself completely true. God has no intention of changing it. Jesus said, "Heaven and earth will pass away, but my words will not pass away" (Matthew 24:35). This reliability of the Bible gives us confidence in our Christian life and in the purpose of the church.

Third, we know that the Bible has *authority*. The Bible speaks with an authority found in no other book in the world. When teachers, police, librarians, referees, or parents make rules, they are using their authority. Many people have some authority over other people. But God has all authority. He has the love, power and wisdom to tell us how best to serve and please Him and each other. He knows. Naturally, His book speaks with

His authority and every word in it has or will some day come true.

The Bible itself tells us of its authority: "All Scripture is *God-breathed* and is useful for teaching, rebuking, correcting and training in righteousness, so that the man of God may be thoroughly equipped for every good work" (2 Timothy 3:16,17). In His Word, God tells us what He wants us to know (*teaching*), what He wants us to stop (*rebuking*), what He wants us to change (*correction*) and how He wants us to live (*righteousness*).

THE BIBLE HAS THREE SPECIAL QUALITIES 1) IT IS COMPLETE 2) IT IS RELIABLE 3) IT HAS AUTHORITY.

The Bible: Alive and Hard at Work

The Bible is a living book—it is alive! That sounds unbelievable doesn't it? But the Bible itself says it is alive: "For the word of God is living and active. Sharper than any double-edged sword, it penetrates even to dividing soul and spirit, joints and marrow; it judges the thoughts and attitudes of the heart" (Hebrews 4:12). Its words are the words of God and they are always true, always at work in the hearts and minds of people who read it. Right now, as your read this chapter,

God's Word is comforting someone who is grieving or in despair. It is strengthening someone else, convincing someone to repent, and teaching another about Jesus Christ. It's at work all over the world, changing people's lives.

But how does the Bible change people's lives? It has special power. Every word of it is correct—what it says about the past, present and future. "As the rain and the snow come down from heaven, and do not return to it without watering the earth and making it bud and flourish, so that it yields seed for the sower and bread for the eater, so is my word that goes out from my mouth: it will not return to me empty, but will accomplish what I desire and achieve the purpose for which I sent it" (Isaiah 55:10-11).

God never lies or exaggerates. He always tells exactly how things are. As people read the Bible they begin to understand its complete honesty. And what they read seems as if it were written exactly for them. They not only learn things about Jesus, but they begin to know Him as a person. His actions, words and the other teachings of the Bible develop a new meaning as people begin to know Jesus more and more. We can meet God and learn from Him in His living book, the Bible. John, who wrote the fourth book in the New Testament said, "Jesus did many other miraculous signs in the presence of his disciples ... but these are written that you may believe that Jesus is the Christ, the Son of God, and that by believing you may have life in his name" (John. 20:30-31).

THE BIBLE HAS SPIRITUAL POWER TO CHANGE PEOPLE.

Tradition and our own sense of what is right are not a sufficient foundation for the life and faith of the people who make up a church. The Bible's complete spiritual teaching, certainty and authority make it our perfect guide. It is God's message to man, full of His love, truth, wisdom and power. It introduces us to Jesus, who can transform the life of anyone who seeks Him by studying and trusting in His Word. The Bible is alive and at work in people around the world.

Things to Do

1. On a sheet of paper, draw and label the shakey foundations on which some people try to build their churches. Draw the one true foundation on which God says His church will be built.

2. Why is the Bible the only reliable guide for finding God's "blueprint" for building His church?

3. How would you explain to

someone your age why you know that Baptist General Conference churches are built on the guidelines laid down in God's Word?

4. What are some changes that obeying the living Word of God has made in your life?

2 More Than a Building

Sharon was hard at work on the quiz when Mrs. Beckstrom came in from the principal's office. She looked up from her paper to see who was in trouble.

Mrs. Beckstrom gave Mr. French a pink slip of paper. He read it and then nodded. Mrs. Beckstrom left quietly, closing the door behind her.

Everyone's eyes were on Mr. French. "Somebody's going to get it," Jimmy whispered, from his seat behind Sharon.

"Sharon, may I see you for a moment?" the teacher asked.

She was shocked. They must have gotten the wrong name. She hadn't done anything wrong.

"Ha, ha, you're in trouble now," Jimmy said, poking her in the back with his pen.

"Me?" she asked, getting up slowly.

Mr. French nodded.

She started towards his desk, an

enormous knot tightening in her throat.

Mr. French smiled slightly as she approached him. "I have a note for you from the office," he said. "You'd better read it."

She took the paper, hands shaking. It said: *I'm waiting in the office. Please come as soon as you can. I've got a big surprise. Dad.*

"Go ahead," Mr. French nodded.

Sharon hurried down the hallway towards the office. She wondered what the surprise was and why her father had to come to school. She had a small idea of what it might be, but that didn't seem possible yet.

Her father and brother were waiting in the office when she opened the door. As soon as she saw their faces she knew her guess had been correct. "Is it a boy or a girl?" she asked excitedly.

"Your new brother, Andrew William, was born at 10:03 this morning," her father said, and hugged her tightly.

Sharon was called out of class to hear great news. Christians have something in common with her. They too have been "called out" to experience great news. And what is that news? "While we were still sinners, Christ died for us" (Romans 5:8).

But what does "called out" mean? And from what are Christians called out?

"You are a chosen people... belonging to God... who called you out of darkness into his wonderful light" (1 Peter 2:9). Christians are people whom God has "called out" from living as sinners, so that they can be part of His holy family. In fact, the word *church* in the New Testament doesn't mean a building or place where people meet. It means "the assembly of called out ones."

ACCORDING TO THE BIBLE, A CHURCH IS THE PEOPLE THEMSELVES.

The "church" is all people who have accepted Jesus Christ as their Lord and received forgiveness of their sins from Him. It includes people from all countries as well as those in the past and future who have become Christians. They are no longer ordinary people; they have Jesus Christ living in their lives. The church is God's family, and each Christian is related to every other Christian through the spiritual life they have received from Christ. No one else is spiritually alive, except those who have accepted Jesus as their Savior and God of their life. "For if you live according to the sinful nature, you will die..." (Romans 8:13). "But if Christ is in you... your spirit is alive because of righteousness" (Romans 8:10).

What Jesus Said About the Church

In the following verses Jesus tells us something very important about the church.

"Who do you say I am?" (Jesus asked His disciples).

Simon Peter answered, "You are the Christ, the Son of the living God."

Jesus replied, "Blessed are you . . . for this was not revealed to you by man, but by my Father in heaven. And I tell you that you are Peter, and on this rock *I will build my church*" (Matthew 16:15-18).

God gave Peter special spiritual knowledge to understand who Jesus was. And then Jesus told him, "I will build my church." Jesus would build it on Peter's faith and spoken belief that Jesus was God's Son and the Savior of mankind. Today He continues to build His church on the faith and spoken belief of Christians who follow Him.

The Bible tells us several important truths about the church. First, because *Jesus is the founder of the church, He is also its foundation.* "For no one can lay any foundation other than the one already laid, which is Jesus Christ" (1 Corinthians 3:11). He is the builder of His church. Christians who serve God help Jesus in the construction of His "assembly of called out ones," but it is Jesus who does the work. He does this through His Word, the Bible, and through the obedience of His servants.

Not only is Jesus the foundation and builder of the church, He is also *Lord* (master) *of the church.* He said, "I will build *my* church." The church belongs to Him. He started it. He changes people by salvation and they become part of His church. "Christ is the head of the church, his body, of which he is the savior" (Ephesians 5:23). The only way the church can be successful as a group of God's people is to obey Christ's commands and permit Him to be the complete master over everything they do together and by themselves.

The Bible tells us that *the church is permanent,* it will always exist. Jesus said, "I will build my church, and the gates of Hades (the power of death) will not overcome it." The church has enemies, but they are not human enemies. Hell, the devil and his demons are trying to destroy the church and its good work, but through Jesus the church will win its battle.

The church is made up of all believers in Jesus Christ no matter where they might be found, in whatever time period or church group. When the New Testament claims that Christ is the head of the church (see Ephesians 5:23), it means that He is the king of believers everywhere. Most often, though, the New Testament speaks of *local assemblies of believers.* And most of Christ's instructions were written to local groups of believers.

The first Christian church was in Jerusalem. After Jesus ascended into heaven, the disciples and other believers "were all together in one place" (Acts 2:1). About 120 people were praying together (see Acts 1:14,15). Then God sent the Holy Spirit to live in them and they began to tell other people about Jesus. As a result of their prayer, the work of the Holy Spirit, and their talking to others about Jesus, 3000 people became part of the local church at Jerusalem in one day.

THE BIBLE SAYS FOUR THINGS ABOUT THE CHURCH: 1) JESUS IS ITS FOUNDER AND BUILDER 2) JESUS IS LORD OF THE CHURCH 3) THE CHURCH IS PERMANENT 4) THE NEW TESTAMENT SPEAKS MOSTLY OF THE LOCAL CHURCH.

What Is a Baptist Church?

What about your church? Where did it get the name "Baptist"?

Many people think that Baptist

churches got their name from John the Baptist. This is not true. The churches of the Baptist General Conference do not claim any one person as their founder, except Christ. The name "Baptist" was a nickname given to people who emphasized the New Testament idea of baptism by immersion instead of the sprinkling of infants with water. But the name Baptist has come to mean a lot more than that.

Baptists believe that each church should make its own decisions and manage its own affairs under the authority of Jesus Christ and the New Testament. They also believe that each individual may communicate directly with God through Jesus Christ. No other person needs to speak for them. Baptists believe that the Bible is the only authority for their faith and actions. These are a few of the beliefs that Baptists uphold, others will be given throughout this book.

The Baptist General Conference is a partnership of over 800 churches who have joined together in order to obey Christ's command for Christians to "go and make disciples of all nations, baptizing them in the name of the Father and of the Son and of the Holy Spirit, and teaching them to obey everything I have commanded you" (Matthew. 28:19,20). The BGC headquarters in Arlington

Heights, Illinois, serves as the central office for missionary outreach, starting churches, publishing and coordination of North American church activities. The Conference also operates Bethel, a Christian college and seminary in St. Paul, Minnesota, and Bethel Seminary—West Campus in San Diego, California. The people in each of these organizations are servants of our churches, helping them to reach our world for Christ.

The New Testament teaches that the church is an "assembly of called out ones." It is people, not a building or place of meeting, which make up a church. The people who make up Baptist churches believe that Jesus started the church, He is its foundation. He owns it and He is building it according to His plan. The church includes all who have received forgiveness for their sins and follow Jesus Christ as their God. The New Testament was written for all Christians, but much of it was written for churches in communities like yours. And your church is part of a united fellowship of over 800 churches, which together seek to share the gospel with all nations. Christ continues to build His church on the faith and spoken belief of those who follow Him.

Things to Do

1. What kind of people are members of the church which God is building now on earth? See 1 Peter 2:9.

2. How would you explain God's plan of salvation to another person, using these Scriptures: Romans 5:8; John 3:16; Habakkuk 1:13a; Romans 3:10, 23; 1 Peter 2:24; Romans 10:9-10?

3. Anyone may belong to the church begun by Jesus Christ, but not everyone does. What must every person believe if he wants to belong to this true church (Matt. 16:13-18)?

4. On a sheet of paper, draw a scriptural church.

a. The church's foundation and builder is . . . (1 Corinthians 3:11).

b. The head who gives direction to the rest of the body is . . . (Ephesians 5:23). How would you draw the top of your church?

c. The church's enemies who will never win their battle against it are . . . (Matthew 16:18). Would they be inside or outside of the church?

d. Individual believers find fellowship in . . . (Acts 2:1). Where would you draw Christians in your picture?

5. If you were making a visual display of your church and its mission in the world, what would you include in the display? Why?

3 A Very Important Idea

Barry's father was one of the busiest men in town. When he wasn't working at the television station, he might be anywhere in town. He did interviews, reported on crimes and accidents and helped open new businesses. Everyone thought that Barry and his sister were pretty lucky to have a famous dad like Wayne Randal. But sometimes Barry wondered if it was really that great.

"Don't bother him," Susan said, as she passed Barry in the hall. "I think he's too busy now."

Barry nervously watched his father from the door of the room. Mr. Randal had books and papers spread out on the desk and was typing at a very fast pace.

"He'll probably get mad," Barry thought, "but I've got to ask."

Mr. Randal looked up as Barry quietly entered the room.

"Would it be OK if I asked you a

question?" Barry asked.

Mr. Randal switched off the typewriter and smiled. "Sure," he said.

"Are you sure I'm not bothering you?" Barry asked.

"Not at all, Barry. I was just finishing up this article so I could spend some time with you and your mother."

"Really?"

Mr. Randal nodded. "What's your question?"

Barry held out the sign-up sheet for the father and son camp out. "Can we go?" he asked. "It'll be great. They have canoeing, fishing, horse riding and underground caves. Can we go, Dad?"

Mr. Randal read the sheet and then glanced at his calendar. "I've already got something scheduled for that weekend," he replied. "I'm afraid I can't get out of it."

Barry's face fell. He turned to leave. "Wait," his father said, "Don't you want to see what's on my calendar?"

Barry took the calendar with a look of disappointment. He turned the page and looked at the weekend in question. His face suddenly lit up. The words *father/son retreat* had been written across Saturday and Sunday.

"You've been planning to go?" Barry asked, elated.

"Ever since it was first mentioned in church," Mr. Randal nodded. "I thought it would be a great way for us to spend more time together."

"Excellent," Barry said, "I can hardly wait."

Mr. Randal was a very busy man, but Barry had personal, direct access to him—he could go right to him because he was his son. This is a very important idea in the thinking of Baptists. We believe that every person has the right to deal personally and directly with God through Jesus Christ. We believe that God has given us this right equally with every other person in the world and in every age. And believe that this right affects the way we treat other people.

What do we mean when we say that everyone has the right to deal personally and directly with God through Jesus? We mean that no one needs to talk to God for you. You can speak to Him yourself, any time you want.

GOD GIVES US THE RIGHT TO SPEAK DIRECTLY TO HIM THROUGH JESUS.

Where Does This Idea Come From?

The New Testament clearly shows that individuals have direct access to God. Jesus was often followed by large crowds. Even though He attracted many people, He always had time to deal with one person at a time. Two good examples of this appear in Luke 8:40-56. Here, even though "the crowds almost crushed him" (because there were so many people), Jesus stopped to heal a sick woman and then visited a man's house in order to raise the man's daughter back to life. Jesus thought each person was important and He let people come directly to Him.

The Bible helps us to see that we have direct access to God. It calls believers priests. According to 1 Peter 2:9, "you are a chosen people, a *royal priesthood,* a holy nation, a people belonging to God, that you may declare the praises of him who called you out of darkness into his wonderful light." Revelation 1:6 says Christ "has made us to be a kingdom and priests to serve his God and Father—"

GOD SAYS EVERY CHRISTIAN IS A PRIEST.

But what does a priest do? The main thing priests have always done is to represent people before God. Instead of a person talking directly to God, a priest would pray for that person, praise God for him and stand in God's presence for him. A priest served God, representing another person to God.

As we have seen, the New Testament teaches that a Christian is himself a priest and therefore doesn't need anyone else to represent him. Every person who desires to has the right to know and talk with God. You never need anyone's permission to speak with God—not your parents, your pastor, your teachers at school or anyone else. God has only one requirement for us to speak with Him, and that is that we know and trust Jesus, His Son.

The Bible says, "there is one God and one mediator between God and men, the man Jesus Christ . . ." (1 Timothy 2:5). When we pray and worship Jesus, we are speaking to God. Jesus hears our thoughts and prayers and tells them to God. Our parents and pastor may pray with us, but they can't pray instead of us. We must be priests to God ourselves.

Making Your Own Choices

Since you can speak directly with God through Jesus Christ, you will be making decisions about Him. What do you think about God? How does He want you to live? How should you relate to other people? The eight subjects that follow are the result of your right to deal personally with God. Baptists believe the Bible gives us instruction for dealing with each subject, but the decision you make about each is a private matter between you and God.

First, it is the special right and responsibility of each person to *read the Bible* or hear it read. By reading and studying the Bible, each person can discover its meaning himself. God desires to speak directly to you through His Word.

Second, every person is responsible for his *own decision of faith in Jesus* and obedience to Him. The Bible says that "to all who received him [Jesus], to those who believed in his name, he gave the right to become children of God" (John 1:12). God wants every person to love Him, accept Jesus and live forever. But He won't force anyone. Nor can anyone else. Everyone must make their own decision whether or not to accept Christ.

Third, each person must decide for himself whether or not to be *baptized.* Only those who have received forgiveness for their sins and accepted Christ as their Lord and Savior should be baptized. Chapter five will give a more complete explanation of this subject.

Each person needs to determine whether or not he should receive the *Lord's Supper.* Neither your church nor family should make this decision for you. But there are some important requirements that anyone must fulfill before receiving the Lord's Supper. Chapter six explains this subject in greater detail.

A person must determine from the Bible *how best to live as a Christian.* How often should you read the Bible? What's the best way to pray? How should you treat people that are mean to you? What does God want you to do today? The Bible will help you find answers to these questions. How you respond to what the Bible says is your own decision.

The right we have to deal directly with God is a right we share with *other people.* Jesus commanded that Christians share their faith with other people, but no one has the right to force anyone to believe or not believe in Christ, or in any other religion.

All church members have the right to *take part in church decisions.* Each person has one vote which he may cast as he thinks best. Even the pastor.

Finally, a Christian's *attitude toward the government* is the result of his direct access to God. The work of the church and the government may overlap at times (for instance, both may be helping starving or homeless people in a city). But neither should attempt to control the activities of the other.

Each of us must determine for

ourself how we will respond responsibly to the privileges we receive from God.

Who Is in Control

Our freedoms work best when they are under the control of Christ. He has given Christians each of these privileges and He can help us be sure we're doing the best thing for God, other people and ourself. Because He is "the head of the body, the church" (Colossians 1:18), Christians must let Him control their lives. When they do, they'll find that their decisions are not as difficult nor the results as costly. We can find out what Jesus expects by reading and studying the New Testament and by listening to Him when we pray.

Jesus' words should control our actions. In Matthew 28:18-19, Jesus commanded all Christians to "go and make disciples of all nations, baptizing them in the name of the Father and of the Son and the Holy Spirit, and teaching them to obey everything that I have commanded you." These two verses are often called the Great Commission. Matthew 22:37-40 is often called the Great Commandment. There, Jesus says, "Love the Lord your God with all your heart and with all your soul and with all your mind . . . Love your neighbor as yourself."

These verses affect the way a Christian will relate to God and to other people. Jesus also wants us to have a good effect on the people we go to church with. We are to be kind, loving, honest and fair. If we are, other people will see that we are different, that we are like Christ.

JESUS WORDS MUST AFFECT THE WAY A CHRISTIAN RELATES TO GOD AND TO PEOPLE.

Christians have a responsibility to God, to the people that make up their church, and to others. They can say with excitement:

"I am free to come to the Lord."

"I am a priest."

"I am responsible to the Lord and to others."

God thinks you are very important. He has given you the right to come directly to Him through Jesus Christ. It's a very important idea. The way we use our freedom should bring praise and glory to God.

Things to Do

1. What do these Scriptures—Luke 8:40-56; 1 Peter 2:9; Revelation 1:6—teach about an individual's direct access to God?

2. What is the one requirement God has for people who want to speak with Him?

3. On a sheet of paper, write down the eight rights of a believer priest (see "Making Your Own Choices"). Beside each right, write one way you will use it so that God will be pleased with you.

4. Find the Great Commission in Matthew 28:18-19 and the Great Commandment in Matthew 22:37-40. Our freedoms work best when they are under Christ's control. How do Jesus' words in the Great Commission and the Great Commandment give us direction in the way we treat

a. God;

b. people who are not Christians;

c. people who are our neighbors;

d. ourselves?

4 Showing You Believe

Andy sat on the bed, surrounded by Lyle's models. There were space battle cruisers and USAF fighters with sweptback wings. There were German tanks, American tanks, two aircraft carriers, several drag cars and a nuclear submarine. It was the best collection of anybody in school. All were well painted with just the right decals and not a spot of glue.

"Well, do you want to join the club?" Lyle asked.

"Yes," Andy answered. "What do I have to do to get in?"

Lyle spun the turret of one of his tanks. "First, you have to own at least five models and you have to have built two in the last six months."

Andy counted back to April, when he had finished the WWII dive bomber. "Okay," he said.

"And you have to pay the dues each week," Lyle said. "Thirty cents."

"For what?" Andy asked.

"To pay for paint," Lyle answered. "You want me to teach you to paint like I do, don't you?"

"Can't I bring my own paint?" Andy asked.

Lyle shrugged. "Yeah, I guess." He though for a minute and said, "There's one more thing you have to do to get into my club."

"What's that?"

"You have to lend me your favorite album for three weeks."

Andy looked at Lyle while he thought. He felt he was being cheated, but he wanted to learn how to paint as well as Lyle.

"Two weeks," he replied, "and no scratches or I quit."

"Welcome to my modelmakers club," Lyle smiled and they exchanged the special handshake.

Andy had to meet several qualifications to become a member of Lyle's club. A church is not a club, but it too has qualifications for membership. To become a member of a Baptist church, a person must meet the following four qualifications. These are based on the example of the churches mentioned in the New Testament.

Spiritual Life

You've probably heard people say that they have been "born again." To many that idea sounds pretty strange. And it did to one of the Jewish leaders in Jesus' time. The man came to see Jesus one night. Jesus told him, "I tell you the truth, no one can see the kingdom of God unless he is born again" (John 3:3). This man had a lot of questions—maybe you have some of the same ones. He asked Jesus, "How can a man be born when he is old?" (verse 4).

Jesus answered, "I tell you the truth, no one can enter the kingdom of God unless he is born of water and the Spirit" (verse 5).

The man was perplexed. "How can this be?" he asked (verse 9).

Jesus answered by talking about Himself, the Son of God. He said that "everyone who believes in [me] may have eternal life. For God so loved the world that he gave his only Son, that whoever believes in him shall not perish but have eternal life" (verses 15, 16).

In short, Jesus told the man that he needed to have a definite experience of faith in Christ (a time when he decided to believe that Jesus is God). Being "born again" is another way of saying we have received spiritual life. Sometimes we refer to this as salvation, conversion, being saved, or having eternal life. Every person has a physical beginning—he or she is born. But Christians have a spiritual beginning too, they are born as eternally living people of God. No one has spiritual life when he is first born, physically. Only God can give spiritual life. "For the wages of sin is death, but the gift of God is eternal life in Christ Jesus our Lord" (Romans 6:23).

EVERY PERSON NEEDS SPIRITUAL LIFE, AND ONLY GOD CAN GIVE IT TO HIM OR HER.

How does a person receive spiritual life in Christ? How does someone become an eternal priest to God? A person *must understand his need.* Unless a person understands that he or she is separated from God by sin, he has no chance of receiving new life. Romans 3:23 says, "For all have sinned and fall short of the glory of God." Sin is disobedience or rebellion against God. No one is perfect except Jesus, who never sinned.

A person must repent of his sins. Each person needs to feel the seriousness of sin and recognize his need to change. It's easy to see other people's faults and think they need to repent, but Jesus said, "Unless you repent, you too will all perish" (Luke 13:3). Repentance is turning away from sin and turning toward God.

A person must ask Jesus for forgiveness and cleansing. 1 John 1:9 tells us, "If we confess our sins, he is faithful and just and will forgive us our sins and purify (clean) us from all unrighteousness (wrongdoing)."

A person must have invited Jesus to take control of his life. It's amazing, but when we ask Jesus to come into our heart, He actually does. He begins to live His life in us, helping us to become more like Himself.

At the moment that Jesus enters a person's life that person is "born again." He or she receives new life. John 1:12 says, "Yet to all who received him, to those who believed in his name, he gave the right to become children of God—" Paul wrote, "That if you confess with your mouth, 'Jesus is Lord,' and believe in your heart that God raised him from the dead, you will be saved" (Romans 10:9).

A person should also give thanks to God for saving his soul. When a Christian thanks God for his salvation, he or she is showing God that he believes God has done what He promised.

Only people who have become Christians by asking for forgiveness and receiving Christ can become members of

Baptist churches.

Telling Others

Sometimes things happen to us that are so great that we have to tell our family and friends. If your team won a softball tournament you'd be excited. You'd want everyone to know. If someone gave you a new ten speed you'd certainly tell your friends right away.

Becoming a Christian is the most important thing that can happen to anyone. Baptists believe the New Testament tells us that we should tell others about our belief in Christ. How else can people know if we've really accepted Christ? In Romans 10:9 Paul says, ". . . if you confess with your mouth, 'Jesus is Lord,' and believe in your heart that God raised him from the dead, you will be saved."

BELIEVERS MUST TALK ABOUT JESUS THEIR LORD.

Baptist churches expect that any person who desires to join in the church's membership will tell people in the church about his faith in Christ and how he came to know Jesus. He may be asked to speak in front to the entire church. Or he may tell a group of church leaders, such as the deacons or elders.

Another Way to Show

Major League baseball players wear special uniforms; so do people in military service. Anyone who sees a person in one of these uniforms immediately knows that that person belongs to a special group. The uniform tells people what you are.

A person who has become a Christian needs to show people that he belongs to Jesus Christ. He does this by being baptized. When a person is immersed (dipped under water) it shows other people that the one baptized belongs to Christ and desires to be like Him. Immersion is a picture of Jesus' death, burial and resurrection. It shows that we are no longer who we used to be, but have received Christ's life in us.

In the New Testament, people who joined the church first received salvation and then were baptized. "Those who accepted his message were baptized, and about three thousand were added to their number (the church) that day" (Acts 2:41).

BELIEVERS ARE BAPTIZED.

Baptist churches follow this pattern by requiring that a person be baptized by immersion as part of becoming a member of the church. Those already

Living a Holy Life

baptized by immersion need not do it again. (You can find out more about this subject in the following chapter.)

In the spring, caterpillars hatch from tiny eggs on the underside of tree leaves. They grow into fat, fuzzy worms, chewing up the leaves. In the summer, they spin a cocoon around themselves. Several weeks later a beautiful moth or butterfly emerges, looking nothing like the original caterpillar. What was once a fat worm is now completely changed, it has been transformed.

When people become Christians they undergo a similar transformation. They change from sinful people, whose sins God hates, to beautifully holy people whom God loves as His own children. Like the caterpillar, they are transformed. Paul described this change in 2 Corinthians 5:17. "Therefore, if anyone is in Christ, he is a new creation; the old is gone, the new is come!"

Christians live differently from other people. They trust in God and realize that they are responsible to Him, to other people and to themselves.

A CHRISTIAN WANTS TO LIVE IN A WAY THAT IS PLEASING TO GOD.

A Christian asks himself, "Will this please God?" before he does something. He doesn't do whatever he feels like doing at the moment.

Baptist churches insist that a person must have received Christ and told others about his faith in order to join in membership of a Baptist church. Also, he must show his new life by being baptized and by beginning to live his new life according to God's standards. All of these requirements come directly from the New Testament.

How the Church Accepts New Members

Once a person has fulfilled the four requirements for membership in a Baptist church, church members vote on whether or not to accept that person as a new member. A person who has met the requirements will be voted into membership. Baptists feel that membership is very important. A member is able to vote on decisions in the church and take part in its ministry. "...the whole body (the church)...builds itself up in love, as each part does its work" (Ephesians 4:16).

If a person has moved into the area and has been a member of another Baptist church, he may move his membership to the new church by bringing a letter of transfer. Again, the church members vote to accept or refuse membership to that person.

After a person has been accepted as a member he is introduced before the entire church (often at a communion service) and the pastor welcomes him into the church family. They pray together, asking God to bless the new member's commitment and responsibilities in the church. After that, the member is expected to support the work of the church with his or her time, talents and possessions.

In summary, to become a member of a church in the Baptist General Conference, a person must have accepted Jesus as his Savior and told others about his faith. He must have already been baptized by immersion and have begun to live by God's standards. When he has met these requirements, he may ask to become a member of the church. He is accepted by vote of the church members.

The local church belongs to Christ, as do all Christian churches. To become part of Christ's church is a great privilege and responsibility. Membership in a church shows you accept that privilege and desire to fulfill your part of the church's responsibilities.

Things to Do

1. Why do Baptist churches insist that people meet their qualifications before they can become members? Does it really matter what else people believe if they have received new life in Jesus?

2. On a sheet of paper, fill in the qualifications and responsibilities of membership in a Baptist church.

Qualifications
- a.
- b.
- c.

Responsibilities
- a.
- b.
- c.

3. Complete these sentences:

a. I know that I have received spiritual life from God because . . .

b. The last time I told someone that Jesus was my Lord was . . .

c. I believe the Bible teaches that baptism shows . . .

5 Showing You Belong

Some things are not easily described. It's hard to say that an oak tree is like a house, a telephone pole, or anything else. An oak tree isn't really like anything else, except other trees. An oak tree is what it is, an oak tree.

Some things in the church are like that, they can only be described by what they are. In the next two chapters you will find out about two things Jesus expects believers to do—one only once and the other frequently. Those two things are not really like anything else, they are simply what they are: baptism and the Lord's Supper.

What Is Baptism?

Baptist churches call both baptism and the Lord's Supper "ordinances" of the church. An ordinance is a regular practice of the church, commanded by Jesus.

Baptists believe that there is a Bible-based method of baptism. We believe that the New Testament clearly shows that baptism is to be done by immersion, lowering a person completely under water. Many other churches do not use this method. They sprinkle water on a person's forehead. But Baptists believe sprinkling is not a Bible-based method for baptism, for the following reasons.

First, the New Testament was originally written in the Greek language. The word *baptism* comes from a Greek word which means "to dip, immerse, submerge or overwhelm." The word baptize is an English language way of saying "immerse." So when we read the word baptize in the New Testament, what it means is to lower someone completely under water.

BAPTISM SHOULD BE BY IMMERSION.

Why do many churches do it the other way? Years ago many people began to think that baptism was necessary for being saved. Some people, like those who were sick, couldn't be immersed. So some church leaders sprinkled water on these people's foreheads. That's how it got started. Hundreds of years later this had become a common practice, and the leaders of many churches made official statements that baptism should be done by sprinkling instead of immersion. This is a good example of people in the church trying to do something the way they think is right and by tradition, rather than trusting the Bible as the only authority for their faith and actions.

We know from the Bible that Jesus Himself was baptized by immersion in the Jordan River. In Matthew 3:16 we read, "As soon as Jesus was baptized, he went up out of the water." Baptists believe that we should continue to baptize people by the method Jesus spoke of in the New Testament—immersion.

Why Be Baptized?

In addition to having been commanded by the Lord Jesus, baptism by immersion has some special meanings. First, it identifies us with Christ and the new life we have received from Him, if we are Christians. "You are all sons of God through faith in Christ Jesus, for all of you who were baptized into Christ have clothed yourself with Christ" (Galatians 3:26,27). Professional athletes wear uniforms that identify them with the rest of the team. Baptism is one way a Christian identifies him- or herself with Christ. Jesus' death, burial and resurrection were very important to Him. Baptism is a picture of those events and shows that the believer finds them personally important to himself. He identifies with them. Baptism also shows a Christian's identification with all other believers.

The second special meaning of baptism is that it shows a Christian has ended his own control of his life and is beginning a new, spiritual life under God's control. "We were... buried with him (Christ) through baptism into death...that, just as Christ was raised from the dead...we too may live a new life" (Romans 6:4). When the believer is lowered under water, it is a picture of Jesus' death and burial for that person's sins. When the person is raised out of the water, this pictures Jesus' resurrection from death. It also shows that the believer has received spiritual life through faith in Him.

BAPTISM BY IMMERSION IS A CLEAR WAY THAT A CHRISTIAN IDENTIFIES HIMSELF OR HERSELF WITH THE DEATH, BURIAL AND RESURRECTION OF THE LORD.

Finally, baptism reminds the believer that he is going to be raised, both body and soul, when Christ returns. When Jesus returns to earth again, those who are saved will join Him in heaven.

Paul described that scene in
1 Thessalonians 4:16. "For the Lord himself will come down from heaven, with a loud command, with the voice of the archangel and with the trumpet call of God, and the dead in Christ (Christians who have already died) will rise first." Not only will a Christian's soul be with God, but he will have a new, perfect body. Baptism by immersion shows that we believe we will be raised with Christ.

Who Should Be Baptized?

You will probably be in a new grade in school next year. You'll be able to do more things on your own and your classes will be harder. In order to begin in a new grade next year, there are requirements you must fulfill this year (getting passing grades on tests, reports, etc.). Anyone who fulfills the requirements will be promoted to a higher grade.

There is one basic requirement that Baptist churches expect a person to fulfill before they are baptized. The person must have asked Jesus for forgiveness and received Him as his Savior and Lord. Faith in Christ must come before baptism or baptism is meaningless. The Bible gives us a good example in Acts 8:12. "But when they believed Philip as he preached the good news of the kingdom of God and the name of Jesus Christ, they were baptized, both men and women." First the people understood Philip's message, then they believed in Jesus and afterwards they were baptized. This pattern of understanding, salvation and then baptism, is consistent throughout the New Testament.

YOU MUST BE "BORN AGAIN" BEFORE YOU CAN BE BAPTIZED.

It follows from this that a person must be old enough to understand how to become a Christian and he or she must have believed in Jesus. You can see that a baby couldn't understand repentance, forgiveness and salvation (see chapter four, "Spiritual Life"). So therefore Baptists do not baptize infants.

Jesus Commands Believers to be Baptized

When we have received Jesus as our Savior, it should be our desire to please Him by obeying His commands. Jesus told His disciples—and all believers since—that they should baptize people who believe in Him. "Then Jesus came to them and said, 'All authority in heaven and on earth has been given to me. Therefore go and make disciples of all nations, *baptizing them in the name of the*

Father and of the Son and of the Holy Spirit, and teaching them to obey everything I have commanded you'" (Matthew 28:19-20). In these verses Jesus tells us that believers should be baptized and they should learn to obey Christ's commands.

It is important that we don't confuse baptism with salvation. Baptism has no power to save us or change us in any way. Receiving Christ as our Lord and Savior is the only way to become a Christian. Baptism is an act of obedience to Christ which shows that we have already been saved. Therefore, no one should be baptized thinking that it will save him or her.

Baptism is an ordinance in Baptist churches. It is something which the Lord commands believers to do. It is a Christian's way of showing other people his or her new life in Christ. It's also a step of loyalty and obedience to Christ. Only believers should be baptized, and then by immersion. Immersion is the New Testament method of baptism and identifies us with Christ in His death, burial and resurrection.

Baptists believe that all believers should be obedient to Jesus' commands and the guiding principles of the New Testament. For this reason we believe that all believers should be baptized. No one should ever force anyone to be baptized against their will. It must be a person's own choice whether or not they will obey the Lord.

Things to Do

1. In your own words, define:
ordinance
baptism
immersion
sprinkling

2. What did Jesus teach about baptism
a. by His example (Matthew 3:16);
b. by His command (Matthew 28:19-20)?

3. Find three special meanings of baptism by immersion:
a. in Galatians 3:26-27
b. in Romans 6:14
c. in 1 Thessalonians 4:16.

4. Complete this sentence: Baptism to me means...

6 When Remembering Is Worship

In the last chapter you read that there are two ordinances given in the New Testament: baptism and the Lord's Supper. Baptism is a picture of the beginning of spiritual life. The Lord's Supper pictures a believer's continuing life with Jesus Christ.

You are probably taller and weigh more than you did last year. You are growing. Your body is changing shape and you are beginning to look more like an adult each year.

Christians who love Jesus and worship Him are growing too. They are beginning to think and act more and more like Jesus in what they do. In their relationship with God. And in how they get along with other people. The Lord's Supper is part of this spiritual growth process.

What Is the Meaning of the Lord's Supper?

Jesus began the Lord's Supper on the night before He was crucified. He gathered His disciples together and told them what was about to happen. They were shocked to hear that one of them would betray Him and that Jesus would be crucified and die. It wasn't at all what they were expecting. When they finished eating together Jesus took the bread, broke it into pieces and gave thanks to God. Then He ate it together with His disciples. Jesus told them that the broken bread was like His body, soon to be broken on the cross for them by nails and a spear. He said they were to remember Him and what He did on the cross, by eating bread together.

He also shared His cup with them and they drank together. He said that the wine was like his blood. His blood was shed for them when he was crucified to make possible the forgiveness of their sins. Again, He asked them to remember him when they shared from the cup together.

Clearly the Lord's Supper is meant to remind us of Jesus as the one who died on the cross for us because of our sins. So when we take communion, we worship Him.

THE LORD'S SUPPER REMINDS US
THAT JESUS DIED FOR OUR SINS.

Most Baptist churches take the Lord's Supper once a month. We need to take the Lord's Supper often enough to be reminded of God's forgiveness, without taking it so often that it becomes meaningless.

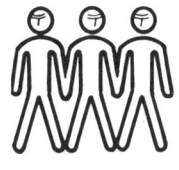

Its Special Meaning

When Jesus spoke of the bread and the cup He said, "...*this is* my body" and "*this is* my blood of the covenant" (Mark 14:22, 24). Baptists believe that the bread and cup *stand for* Jesus' body and blood. His body, like bread, was broken. His blood, like the juice, was poured out when He died on the cross. Both bread and juice remind us of Christ's great sacrifice for us.

We recognize that in many churches the Lord's Supper is called communion. Communion means having things in common and sharing them.

When we take part in the Lord's Supper we are joined in communion with other believers. It is a holy time *together* in God's presence.

There is another important meaning of the Lord's Supper. It is a way to preach about Christ. According to Paul the apostle, "...whenever you eat this bread and drink this cup, you proclaim the Lord's death until he comes" (1 Corinthians 11:26). Every time people in a church take the Lord's Supper, their doing so speaks about Christ's death for mankind. Christians are reminded that they have been saved by faith in Christ's death for them. Non-Christians see what Christ's death means to those who have accepted Him.

Who Should Take the Lord's Supper?

We can answer this question several ways. A person should know Jesus Christ as Savior and be seeking to live for Him before they take the Lord's Supper. It is impossible to share in deep friendship and understanding with God and His church if we do not first have a personal relationship with Him through Christ. A person must carefully decide for himself if he or she really is a Christian before deciding to take part in the Lord's Supper.

ONLY A "BORN AGAIN" BELIEVER SHOULD TAKE THE LORD'S SUPPER.

Another condition for the Lord's Supper is that we cannot have unconfessed sin in our lives. The New

Testament is very clear in explaining this to us.

> Therefore, whoever eats the bread or drinks the cup of the Lord in an unworthy manner will be guilty of sinning against the body and the blood of the Lord. *A man ought to examine himself before he eats of the bread and drinks of the cup.* For anyone who eats and drinks without recognizing the body of the Lord eats and drinks judgement on himself (1 Corinthians 11:27-29).

The words "examine himself" in these verses do not mean inspecting one's body. What they mean is that a person who takes the Lord's Supper should face up to the things he might have said or done, or is doing, which displease God. A good way to do this is to pray and ask God to show you any sin in your life. That sin might be anger at someone else, having cheated or stolen something. It could be lying, disobedience to parents, breaking the law, or anything else which displeases God. Whatever the sin, it must be confessed to God and the person must ask for forgiveness.

A person who knows they have sinned and does not ask for forgiveness before taking communion, brings "judgment on himself." To do so invites

God's discipline.

Jesus Wants Believers to Receive the Lord's Supper

In the last chapter you read that Jesus commanded His followers to be baptized and to baptize others. He also told them to take the Lord's Supper, when He said "do this in remembrance of me" (Luke 22:19). The disciples passed this ordinance on to the first Christian churches. In 1 Corinthians 11:23 Paul says, "For I received from the Lord what I also passed on to you..." He went on to describe the Lord's Supper, which he "passed on" to them. Receiving the Lord's Supper is a way to show Jesus our love for Him. It's a way to worship Him and remember His death for us. It's a way to be close with Him. It shows our loyalty to Christ and proclaims the importance of His death for us.

JESUS COMMANDED HIS FOLLOWERS TO TAKE THE LORD'S SUPPER.

Things to Do

1. What does baptism picture or illustrate (Romans 6:4)?

2. What picture does God want us to have through the Lord's Supper?

3. In the section of this chapter called

"It's Special Meaning," find three important facts about the Lord's Supper.

4. Who should take the Lord's Supper? Who should not?

5. Read Luke 22:19 now. Then, next time you are at the Lord's Supper, what should you think about?

7 Keeping Things in Order

Coach McHeney waved Ryan off the bench. "Go in for Kerry at center," he said.

Ryan could hardly believe it. He hadn't played in several games and was beginning to think the team was better off without him. Now Kerry had twisted his ankle and Ryan was going to be in the playoffs. It seemed too good to be true.

It was a close game and as Ryan came on court he felt he would either save or ruin the team. He remembered coach McHeney's pregame instructions: "You've got to play aggressive with these guys. You've got to beat them at the net and control the ball. If you try to show off or take outside shots they'll beat you. But if you control the ball as a team we'll be in the semi-finals next week. It's up to you."

Scott passed the ball in to Ryan, who drove down-court. They passed several times and then hit Dave under the net. He tried a jump shot but missed.

The other team got the rebound and the forward streaked in to make a fast layup. That put them ahead by three.

Ryan glanced to the bench where coach McHeney was shaking his head.

Ryan led the next play, working the ball to the outside. He passed to Scott, who cut up the middle and then got called on a foul.

The other team made the first free throw but missed on the second. Ryan got the ball near the outside and made a long shot. The instant the ball left his hands he remembered the coach's words: "If you take outside shots they'll beat you." He felt angry at himself, but then the ball arced downward and —swish— fell through the net.

"Made it!" Ryan shouted. He usually shot best from the outside.

The other team called a timeout. Ryan's team went to the sidelines for final instructions.

"Good shot, Ry—," Scott said, slapping Ryan's palm.

"Great shot," Dave echoed.

"We've got a little over a minute to play and we're down by two," the coach said. "Stick to tight ball control but with one exception. Feed Ryan on the outside; they're weak there and it looks like he's hot. Otherwise, same game plan, OK? Let's get 'em."

The last minute of the game was exhilarating. Ryan made two out of three shots from the outside and Scott and Dave made inside shots. When the buzzer sounded, they were up by two points. Dave sunk the winning basket which put them in the semi-finals.

The whole team was buzzing with excitement. Everyone had done their part. Dave had put the last shot through the hoop but he hadn't won the game. They all had.

As in the story above, it's usually the best-working team that wins championship games. Everyone is important, everyone does their part. The coach provides the game plan and the team works together, using everyone's strengths to seek a single purpose—the team's success.

Baptist churches are organized something like a team. Jesus has provided the instruction through His Word, the Bible. He works specifically with each member on the team, using their special abilities for His glory. And each member of the team works with other members to achieve God's purpose for the church—spreading the good news of Jesus Christ to the entire world.

Teams must be organized to be effective. That is, everyone must understand where he fits in and what needs to be done. The church also needs to be organized. Jesus gave no special commands about how the church should be organized. But we can see that the New Testament emphasizes the importance of the local group, the people who worship together in one place. To maintain order and progress in these groups, an organizing plan is necessary.

CHURCHES MUST BE ORGANIZED TO BE EFFECTIVE.

Local Leaders

The New Testament mentions two special jobs that exist in every church. They are *pastor* and *deacon*. The pastor is described in several ways. Sometimes he is called a shepherd, sometimes a bishop or elder. All of these refer to the position of a pastor. He cares for the people as a shepherd cares for his flock. He has a primary responsibility for teaching and managing in the church. Many churches have more than one man who carry out the duties of a pastor.

Pastors have several main responsibilities in a local church. A basic task is to "prepare God's people for works of service." This work includes preaching and teaching the Word of God. Paul described this in Ephesians 4:11-12 when he said, "It was he who gave some to be apostles, some to be prophets, some to be evangelists, and some to be pastors and teachers, to prepare God's people for works of service, so that the body of Christ may be built up..."

The pastor has a part in guiding the life of the church. He is a partner with other members and is equal with them when the church votes on a major decision. But pastors generally guide the day to day work of the church.

In many places the Bible describes a pastor as a shepherd; one who is responsible for the care of people in the church. He often visits people or helps them discuss problems. This part of a pastor's work is described in Acts 20:28. "Keep watch over yourselves and all the flock of which the Holy Spirit has made you overseers. Be shepherds of the church of God, which he bought with his own blood." The pastor doesn't take the place of Jesus as leader of the church. He is a person who has been asked by the Lord and the people who make up the church to help them learn about and follow God. He has been chosen for this purpose and has received special training for this kind of work.

What Are Deacons?

The other local church leaders mentioned in the New Testament are deacons. We believe that Acts 6 describes how the job of deacon began. The apostles (who had been with Jesus) were very busy as the church grew larger and larger. There were a group of Greek widows who were not getting any food. So the Greek Jews spoke to the apostles about it. The apostles couldn't do everything, so they said, "Brothers, choose seven men from among you who are known to be full of the Spirit and wisdom. We will turn this responsibility over them and will give our attention to prayer and the ministry of the word" (Acts 6:3,4). The seven who were selected show us how deacons worked in that church. The word deacon means servant.

There are of course many ways to serve Christ in the church, and so there are many other servants in most churches. Some are teachers, secretaries, trustees, treasurers, missions and music leaders, etc. Each church decides what jobs are necessary for them to do the work Christ calls them to do.

Who Makes Decisions In the Church?

In your family, decisions are probably made differently at different times. You probably don't have the final say if your family is buying a new car. But you may decide how to spend your allowance or earnings. There may be some decisions (such as what to do for entertainment) where everybody has an equal say and the majority wins. This last method of making decisions is called democracy, which you recognize as our country's system of government.

Baptists believe that everyone in the church has equal opportunity and that believers are priests to God. For these reasons, our churches are democracies. Every member has an equal say in major decisions of the church. No one, not even the pastor, has more "votes" than anyone else. Jesus Christ is the head of the church, overseeing everything.

How Jesus Controls Church Democracy

Every airport has a flight controller. His or her job is to control when and where planes land and take off, so that none collide. A pilot may decide to land without the controller's instructions, but he endangers himself and many passengers by so doing.

Jesus controls the operation of the church. People may try to run it on their own without seeking or obeying His directions, but their work will prove ineffective or harmful unless it is brought under His control.

Jesus has set several guidelines for

churches to follow as democracies, which you will recognize from earlier chapters. First, the New Testament is the authority for a church's actions and decisions— not the ideas of people in the church, no matter how wise these ideas may appear. Second, each person is responsible to work for the common good of the entire church. No one should try to get his or her way if it will cause trouble between church members. Not even the pastor. Third, Jesus has given the church a basic task. That task is to spread the gospel to all nations, baptizing people and teaching them to be like Christ. This also controls how the church government works, and the church must work together in unity to achieve this goal.

BAPTIST CHURCHES ARE DEMOCRACIES, AND JESUS IS THE HEAD OF THE CHURCH.

Things to Do

1. Circle the words the Bible uses to describe a pastor's work:
shepherd   boss   bishop
layman   elder   overseer

2. Find several duties of a pastor given in the section called "Local Leaders" and list them below:
a. (Ephesians 4:11-12)

b.

c.

d. (Acts 20:28)

    3. Complete this sentence: The word deacon means . . .

    4. Baptist churches are democracies, and Jesus is the Head of the church. List the guidelines to follow that Jesus has set for church democracies.

8 A Secret You Can't Keep

"Red light," Amy said.

Her mother stopped the car at the intersection and waited for the light to change. Amy tapped her feet on the floorboard. She could hardly wait to get to Kendra's house. They always had a fantastic time when Amy slept over.

Suddenly there was a terrible screeching of tires and a blaring horn. Amy stared in amazement. A blue car was trying to turn left but was blocking an oncoming station wagon. It all happened very fast and yet to Amy it looked like slow motion.

The front end of the station wagon veered to the right to avoid broadsiding the turning car. Suddenly it was smashed from behind by a yellow Cadillac. The Cadillac pushed the station wagon into the side of the blue car with a tremendous thud, lifting one side off the ground momentarily. Glass exploded and hub caps bounced off the two cars. Broken trim fell to the ground and station wagon's front fender was torn to jagged chunks. The side of the blue car was caved in.

Several cars stopped, squealing their tires to avoid hitting the three wrecks.

Amy's heart was pounding. She watched the man in the Cadillac climb out and run to the station wagon. He helped the driver out and they both tried to pry open the doors of the blue car. Both were jammed shut.

"She's hurt! Someone call an ambulance," the Cadillac driver shouted. A gas station attendant ran into his office to place the call.

In a very short time a fire truck, police car and ambulance arrived, lights flashing. A policeman directed traffic. Amy's mother pulled into the gas station and parked.

"Are we staying?" Amy asked.

"We have to," her mother answered, "we witnessed the accident."

The firemen used an air chisel to open the door of the blue car. The paramedics carefully removed a middle-aged woman from the front seat and placed her on a stretcher. In a few minutes they were headed for the hospital, siren screaming.

A police officer approached Amy

and her mother, clipboard in hand. He introduced himself and asked them both to describe what happened. He drew a sketch from what they told him and said that they might be called as witnesses in court. Then he left.

When it was all over, they continued on to Kendra's house. Amy was still shaking from the shock of the accident. She hoped the lady in the ambulance would be all right.

Amy had seen something very sad and important happen, and she wanted to tell other people about. It had had a powerful effect on her and she couldn't help but tell Kendra, the policeman and others. She was a witness and she needed to share with other people what she had experienced.

Christians have had something happen to them that is even more dramatic than what happened to Amy. They have received God's Spirit living inside of them. They have been saved from being condemned by God, through their faith in Jesus Christ's death, burial and resurrection for them. Because of the new life they have received, they are witnesses of what God has done. And "witnesses" want to tell unsaved people so that they too can meet and receive forgiveness from Jesus Christ. In fact, that is a main responsibility of the church.

JESUS COMMANDED THE CHURCH TO TELL THE WORLD ABOUT HIMSELF.

The Church's Main Job

The church was founded with a job to do. This is obvious from Jesus' last statements to His disciples. In Acts 1:8 it is written that He said, "...you will be my witnesses in Jerusalem, and in all Judea and Samaria, and to the ends of the earth." Those who followed Him were to tell people in their own country, neighboring lands and the rest of the world. In chapter three we read some other things Jesus said about the church's job: "Therefore go and make disciples of all nations, baptizing them in the name of the Father and of the Son and of the Holy Spirit, and teaching them to obey everything I have commanded you" (Matthew 28:19-20). Here again, Jesus commanded the church to tell the world about Himself and help people become Christians.

Only Jesus can keep unsaved people from dying as sinners. That's why He wants the church to spread the message of the Gospel—God's good news. He told His disciples, "I am the way and the truth and the life. No one comes to the Father except through me" (John 14:16). He loves every person, no matter what they are like or what they believe. And He wants everyone to become a Christian. "He is patient with you, not wanting anyone to perish, but everyone to come to repentence" (2 Peter 3:9). Jesus wants every Christian and the church as a whole to tell unsaved people about His great love for them.

The Need of the World

God's heart is breaking because people need Him and don't know Him. We see proof of this many places in the New Testament. In Matthew 9:35-38, for example:

> Jesus went through all the towns and villages, teaching in their synagogues, preaching the good news of the kingdom and healing every disease and sickness. When he saw the crowds, *he had compassion* [deep sympathy or sorrow] *on them,* because they were harassed and helpless, like sheep without a shepherd. Then he said to his disciples, "The harvest is plentiful but the workers are few. Ask the Lord of the harvest, therefore, to send out workers into his harvest field."

Jesus was very concerned about people. He told them about God, healed their sicknesses and felt deep sorrow that so many people didn't know God.

The world needs to hear about Jesus. In fact, current population statistics tell us that by the last part of the twentieth century, there will be over 4.7 billion people on earth. The majority are not Christians. In fact, less than one third of that number will know Jesus. What do these numbers mean? If you walked down your street and counted two out of every three houses, and then did the same for every street in your town, you'd begin to get an idea of how many people are left out. The whole world is like that. An overwhelming majority of people alive today do not know the God who loves them.

THE WHOLE WORLD NEEDS TO HEAR ABOUT JESUS.

God Uses People

God uses people to lead other people to Christ. There is no other way. Paul wrote to the church at Rome:

> Everyone who calls on the name of the Lord will be saved. How, then, can they call on the one they have not believed in? And how can they believe in the one of whom they have not heard? An how can they hear without someone preaching to them? And how can they preach

unless they are sent? As it is written, "How beautiful are the feet of those who bring the good news!" (Romans 10:13-15)

According to these verses, Christians must go to other people and preach about Christ. If not, non-Christians will not have the chance to believe in Jesus, ask for salvation and be saved. Unless somebody says something, nobody receives Christ.

GOD WANTS US TO BRING THE GOOD NEWS OF CHRIST TO OTHER PEOPLE.

His Command to Us

In the Bible, Christ commands believers to tell the world about Him. He commands Christians to *make disciples of all nations.* This means churches are to help people everywhere become Christians. They do this two ways: through individuals and through organizations. Every Christian is responsible to Jesus for sharing his or her faith with people who don't know Jesus or believe He is God. All members are different, but all are needed to accomplish the job. Different people will have different ways to tell other people and varying opportunities to do so. Every Christian should tell non-Christians he knows, as God gives him the opportunity.

Christians are also responsible to tell people beyond their local area about Christ. They can do this by joining together in a mission organization, where churches work together to train people and send them to other countries to serve the Lord. The group of churches that make up our Baptist General Conference have two organizations for this purpose. The Home Missions Board starts new churches and supports existing churches all across North America. The World Missions Board works in Mexico, South America, Asia, Africa, Japan and the Philippines. These organizations help local churches reach out to the whole world for Jesus.

Jesus commands Christians to *baptize* believers in the name of God. Christians need to help those who have not been baptized to understand why it is important and what it means. (You can review this topic in chapter five.) This requires patient training of people who have become Christians.

Jesus commands Christians to *teach* people about Himself, the Bible and obedience to Christ. God wants every Christian to grow up to be honest, just, holy and loving, like Jesus. He wants Christians to be as close to perfect as possible so that people will know them and see what God is like. Paul spoke of this in Colossians 1:28. "So, naturally, we proclaim Christ! We warn everyone we meet, and teach everyone we can, all that we know about him, so that we may bring every man up to his full maturity in Christ" (Phillips). The purpose of this teaching is to develop Christians who know what they believe and live according to what the Bible teaches.

Sunday school, clubs, vacation Bible school, the pastor's message, home Bible studies, Christian camping and many other methods are used by churches to teach people about Jesus, the Bible and the Christian life.

Teaching is also important in the work of world missions. The missionary teaches and trains people in other countries who do most of the local work themselves. Often the methods listed above are used by missionaries, as they teach about Christ.

JESUS COMMANDED CHRISTIANS TO MAKE DISCIPLES IN ALL NATIONS, BAPTIZING AND TEACHING THEM.

The church has a job to do. It is to tell the whole world about Jesus, baptizing believers and teaching them to obey Christ. The Lord has commanded the church to make disciples of all nations. People are hurting in many ways and

Jesus is the only one who can heal their souls. It is the Christian's job to share Jesus with his neighbors and people all across the world. It's a tough job, but people need to hear so that they can believe. They need a "witness" to tell them about the love and forgiveness of God.

Do you know Jesus? Have you told anyone about Him recently?

"He is patient with you, not wanting anyone to perish, but everyone to come to repentence."

Things to Do

1. What makes a person a witness?

2. What is the church's main job on earth (Matthew 28:19-20; John 14:16; 2 Peter 3:9)?

3. Draw a circle to represent the earth. Draw a vertical line ⅓ of the way across. Are you part of the ⅓ of the world who know Jesus Christ as Savior or do you belong to the more than ⅔ of the world who don't know Him (Romans 10:13-15)?

4. If you belong to the ⅓, you are part of the church—a part of those people who have a secret too good to keep to themselves. What is God's plan for reaching the more than ⅔ of the world who don't know Him (Romans 10:13-15)?

5. What person could you witness to this week?

9 Taking Care of Borrowed Stuff

Kevin had to hurry, he was already late for band practice. He rushed down the hall, wondering what Mr. Worster would say. His clarinet case was banging against his leg.

When he opened the door, several band members looked at him, the clock, and back at him again. So did the band leader.

Kevin's face reddened. He hoped that Mr. Worster wouldn't yell at him in front of the class. He circled around the back of the room and slid down into his seat. His heart was pounding.

He quickly placed the sheet music on his stand and flipped up the latches of his clarinet case. When he raised the lid the bare red velvet lining stared up at him. It was gone! His clarinet was gone!

"Oh, no," he cried.

"What is it, Kevin?" the band leader

asked. He was one of the most popular teachers in the school.

"My clarinet—" Kevin gasped, "it's gone!"

"Are you sure?" Mr. Worster asked, coming down the aisle.

"It's not in the case," the girl on Kevin's right confirmed.

"We'd better go to my office," Mr. Worster advised. He called in another teacher to take his place while they were gone.

Kevin closed the case and got up slowly. He felt frightened and confused. What would his mom and dad say if they found out about the clarinet? They had rented it from Grant's Music store. It wasn't even his and he had already lost it. But how? He had it when he got on the bus. How did it disappear? His hands were shaking as these questions chased through his mind.

In the band leader's office Mr. Worster asked, "Is there anyone on the bus who might want to scare you or play a trick on you?"

Kevin immediately thought of Jimmy. He was always bothering somebody, pulling pencils out of their pockets or pounding on their arm with his knuckles. He often teased Kevin about his freckles.

"Yes," Kevin replied hesitantly. "Do I

have to tell his name?"

Mr. Worster shook his head. "I think I have a good idea already," he replied.

Kevin then remembered what had happened. He was sitting about a third of the way up from the back of the bus. He slid the case under the seat as the bus started up. Jimmy got on two stops later and called Kevin "Carrothead." He sat down two seats behind Kevin and immediately began to poke Randy in the back of the neck. When they got to school, Kevin looked for the case under the seat but it had been moved. He found it in the back of the bus. But he had no idea that Jimmy or someone else would have opened it and taken the clarinet.

Kevin got his clarinet back later that day. The janitor had found it wrapped in a jacket and stuck in a bush by the front door of the school. Someone had played a cruel joke on him.

Kevin learned a hard lesson about taking care of things entrusted to him. He knew that he was responsible for Mr. Grant's clarinet and that he would have to answer for what happened to it. These ideas of being entrusted with someone else's property, using it wisely and having to answer for its use or abuse, can be summed up in the New Testament word *stewardship*.

The Bible says that Christians are to

be good "stewards." Today we call stewards managers. And we must be good managers of everything that God has entrusted to us. "Now it is required that those who have been given a trust must prove faithful" (1 Corinthians 4:2). We have been entrusted with special abilities, time and money.

CHRISTIANS MUST BE GOOD MANAGERS OF EVERYTHING GOD HAS ENTRUSTED TO THEM.

Special Abilities Come from God

Are there some things you do better than your friends or other people you know? Some people are good at sports, others have musical talent, some draw, paint or write well. Some are funny and others very intelligent or friendly. All our talents and special abilities are a gift from God. "But each man has his own gift from God; one has this gift, another has that" (1 Corinthians 7:7). These abilities belong to the Lord and He has entrusted them to us.

We know a Christian's special abilities belong to the Lord and must be used by him for three reasons.

The first reason we know a Christian's special abilities belong to the Lord is because the Bible teaches us that *He has given us those abilities.* This is stated in Romans 12:6. "God has given each of us the ability to do certain things well" (TLB). The skills we have and the health, time, energy and opportunities to develop our abilities are all God-given. He has entrusted them to us to be used for His glory.

Second, *Christians no longer belong to themselves,* they belong to God. "You are not your own; you were bought at a price [Jesus' death]. Therefore honor God with your body" (1 Corinthians 6:19-20).

A slaveowner back before the Civil War bought a slave. The next day he went to the house where she was living. When he arrived, she looked at him sadly and said, "I am ready to go." The man answered, "I do not want you to go with me. I bought you in order to set you free." She was so amazed at the thought of being free that she couldn't speak. Finally, she replied, "Then I will be your servant forever." That is the way it is for people who know Jesus as their Lord. They don't serve Him because they have to, but because they love Him and are grateful for what he has done for them.

The third reason for a Christian to use the ability that God has given him or her is because of *the needs of the world and the needs of the church.* We studied the needs of the world in the previous chapter. Those needs are only met by

Jesus Christ. It is the church's job to tell the world about Him. The church is only able to do this as those who make up the church give our special abilities, time and the things we own to be used in the church's ministry (service to others). The apostle Paul was a good example of this attitude. In Romans 1:9 he talks about *"God, whom I serve with my whole heart in preaching the gospel of his Son..."*

OUR BEST ABILITIES AND EFFORTS BELONG TO GOD. THEY HAVE BEEN ENTRUSTED TO US AND SHOULD BE GIVEN TO CHRIST AND THE WORK OF HIS CHURCH.

Got a Minute?

If you are like me, some days are so long and boring that it seems as if they will last forever. Other days are so much fun that they are almost over before they begin. Time is a pretty strange thing when you think about it. But everybody gets the same dose. Presidents and Prime Ministers, with their many responsibilities, have the same amount of time as you do, or even as a baby with no responsibilities. The important thing about time is what you do with it.

The Bible emphasizes that Christians must use their time well. Jesus told His disciples, "As long as it is day, we must do the work of him who sent me. Night is coming, when no one can work" (John 9:4). While believers are alive they are to use their time to serve God. When the world ends, the time will be run out for doing anything.

Time is an opportunity. We can use it for God and the work of His church, or we can use it selfishly on ourselves. Paul told the believers in Ephesus, "Be very careful, then, how you live—not as unwise but as wise, making the most of every opportunity, because the days are evil" (Ephesians 5:15,16). How do you use your time? How much TV do you watch? How much time are you doing nothing? How many hours do you sleep? Are you on time when you go places? Does the Lord control how you use your time? How much of it?

CHRISTIANS ARE TO BE GOOD MANAGERS OF THEIR TIME.

What About Your Treasure?

There are a lot of stories about buried treasure. Captain Kidd, a British pirate, was supposed to have buried his loot in a hidden location. The Lost Dutchman Mine, an amazingly wealthy gold mine, is somewhere in America's great southwestern region. Sunken ships off the east coast hide buried riches from Spain, England and France. Many people wish they could find these missing treasures buried in the earth or sea.

Jesus said, "Do not store up for yourselves treasures on earth, where moth and rust destroy, and where thieves break in and steal. But store up for yourselves treasures in heaven...For where your treasure is, there your heart will be also" (Matthew 6:19-21). Whatever is most valuable to you is your treasure.

God owns everything, even the money we have. It comes from Him. He wants all believers to use part of their money for His work.

You've probably heard of the idea of *tithing* (giving one tenth of what you earn to God, for His work). This can be a good guide for our giving, although it is not the only guide. The important thing is that we will be in the practice of giving so other people's needs will be met. Paul told the believers in Corinth, "Whoever sows sparingly will also reap sparingly, and whoever sows generously will also reap generously. Each man should give what he has decided in his heart to give, not reluctantly or under compulsion (by force), for God loves a cheerful giver" (2 Corinthians 9:6,7). Every Christian needs to be a giver.

When we give to the Lord's work we

show a lot about our Christian life. We show that Jesus is our Master. We show that we honor God's Word, which teaches us to give. We show love, the same kind of love that moved God to give His Son for us. We show we're thankful for God's goodness and we show we care about doing the work Jesus has entrusted to us.

A Christian who gives part of his or her possessions for the Lord's work helps the church do its job of fulfilling the Great Commission. A Christian's gifts to the church help support the work of mission organizations in the United States and other countries. The mission work of our own Baptist General Conference continues to expand as people in our churches feel led by the Lord to pray and give money.

The Bible suggests a helpful way for Christians to give money to the Lord's work. "On the first day of every week, each one of you should set aside a sum of money in keeping with his income, saving it up..." (1 Corinthians 16:2). A person who does this will contribute to the work of the church every week. This will help missions to continue to do the work given them by God. Every person needs to be in a sharing relationship with Jesus Christ and other people. Giving money to people who "witness" in other countries doesn't mean that the Christian shouldn't witness where he is. But he can do part of the work by giving of his possessions to the mission of the church.

A PART OF OUR MONEY IS TO BE USED FOR GOD'S WORK THROUGH HIS CHURCH.

Everything that a person has and is comes from God. God allows us to use the special abilities, time and possessions He has given so that we might work for His glory. Baptists believe that every Christian should strive to be a good caretaker of what God has given him. This includes things he does well, how he spends his day and what he does with what he owns. A Christian realizes that he or she no longer belongs to himself. He has been bought with Christ's blood. He serves God not because he has to, but because he loves Him and is grateful to Him. And as he is a generous giver, God is generous with him.

Things to Do

1. Define the New Testament word "stewardship." What is a modern word for the same thing?

2. Find three reasons why a Christian should use his or her special abilities for the Lord:
a. in Romans 12:6

b. in 1 Corinthians 6:19-20
c. in Romans 1:9

3. Read John 9:4 and Ephesians 5:15-16. Make a time chart showing how you spend your time in an average day. In your judgment, are there some better ways you could use your time?

4. List the things you spend money on. After reading 2 Corinthians 9:6-7, do you think you're getting the most for what you spend?

10 You've Got Connections

It hardly seemed possible that Grandpa Willis could be dead. He had been so full of fun eight months earlier, when Amy had last seen him. The whole family had visited Grandma and Grandpa Willis while on vacation. Now as she stared at the man in the silk-lined casket, Amy couldn't help but think that Dick Willis might suddenly sit up and say, "Land sakes, you folks are as gullible as ever!"

But Dick Willis did not stir. And Grandma seemed heartbroken. Later that day, Amy, her mother, father and Grandma Willis were all sitting at Grandma's table. All were silent, in respect for Grandma. There was a knock at the door and Amy's father got up to answer.

Two women and a man came in, each carrying a dish.

"Hello, Ellie, I'm sorry to hear about Dick," the first woman said, from the adjoining room.

"Come in," Grandma Willis

motioned.

Amy recognized the three people immediately. Whenever her family had visited her grandparents they always attended the local Baptist church, where Grandma and Grandpa Willis were members. They had become familiar with several people in the church, including the three visitors.

Ellie Willis introduced her children and grandchild to the church members.

When the introductions were over, the man said, "We didn't want to disturb you, Ellie, but we thought we could save you a little trouble with dinner. So we fixed a few things to tide you through."

"You're such good friends," Grandma Willis replied. "I don't know what I'd do without you." She struggled to hold back her tears.

"The Lord has blessed us all through your husband," the man replied. "He was a godly and generous man." The women nodded and left their dishes on the counter top.

"We'll stop in tomorrow," the first woman said. They left quietly.

"That was very kind of them," Amy's mother said.

"They've become almost as close as family to me," Grandma Willis replied.

The atmosphere was somewhat cheered as they dug into the meat pie, baked potatoes and cookies that the church friends had prepared. Amy could see that her grandmother had been comforted by the kind action. She was glad that such loving people would be consoling Grandma when she and her parents had to leave. They would help her feel less alone.

Christians naturally share their lives with other Christians. As part of God's family, they have many things in common. When they show the things they have in common, because they belong to Jesus, they have fellowship with each other. Fellowship takes place when Christians worship or pray together. When they tell each other about the Lord's work in their lives, or join together to do God's work. When they share interests, feelings, loyalty and friendship. People who have fellowship share their life in Christ. As a result, they accept, support, encourage and care for each other.

As in the story above, Christians not only have fellowship in their own church. But, because of Christ, they can have fellowship with Christians everywhere.

Fellowship in Local Churches

Local churches are important for believers because there they can gather together and find support in their mutual need for fellowship. When people moved from other countries to America, they often joined communities of people from their former land. They had much in common already and they enjoyed many of the same cultural interests. In a similar way, Christians are drawn to other Christians in their local churches.

This was true in Old Testament times. Wherever the Hebrew people went, they would gather to worship together. Until the temple was built in Jerusalem, they worshiped together outside God's holy tent, the tabernacle. When the temple was destroyed and the people forced to move to many different countries, they established a synagogue (local assembly) wherever they went. There, they shared in worship and fellowship with other Jews.

In the New Testament we read that Christ went to the synagogue regularly on the Sabbath. The churches of the first century came together for fellowship, meals and worship. The fact that many of the New Testament letters (Romans through 2 Thessalonians) were written to local churches shows the importance God places on fellowship. The writer of Hebrews warned believers against neglecting being together. He said, "Let us not give up meeting together, as some are in the habit of doing, but let us encourage one another—" (Hebrews 10:25).

Fellowship in a local church also gives believers a sense of security. They know that things they have in common with other Christians in the church will last. They know that the friendships they form with other Christians will exist even after they die, when they fellowship together in heaven. Jesus said, "I will build my church, and the gates of Hades (death) will not overcome it" (Matthew 16:18).

One more thing is important about the fellowship of the local church. It provides opportunities for Christians to serve God together. The Bible says that every believer has a specific God-given ability which the rest of the church needs. Each person is different, but the special abilities of all are needed to work together. "Just as each of us has one body with many members, and these members do not all have the same function, so in Christ we who are many form one body, and each member belongs to all the others. We have different gifts, according to the grace given us" (Romans 12:4-6).

GOD WANTS CHRISTIANS TO HAVE FELLOWSHIP WITH EACH OTHER.

Bigger Fellowship

Some things are much bigger than they first appear to be. Mountains in the distance never look as large as they do up close. And it's really not until you get to the top of one that you realize how many there are and how far apart they are. They look much greater than when you saw them from far away.

The church is also much larger than it appears to be. It's very easy to think only of the church you attend or other churches you've been to. But your church is part of a group of about 800 churches, which we call the Baptist General Conference. The churches in our Conference work together for three main reasons.

First, we are in fellowship together to show that we are not alone in our beliefs, but that many other churches share our same convictions. In Ephesians 4:4-6, Paul spoke of the basic things all Christians share. He said, "There is *one body* and one Spirit—just as you were called to one hope when you were called—one Lord, *one faith,* one baptism; one God and Father of all, who is over all and in all and through all." Paul says here that there is one church (body) of which every Christian is a member. This is true because all Christians share faith in the same Lord, Jesus Christ. Your church is part of this bigger fellowship of churches.

Second, the churches of the Baptist General Conference share in the *same interests,* and therefore can help each other in their work. A good example of this occurs in the book of Acts. "While they were worshiping the Lord and fasting, the Holy Spirit said, 'Set apart for me Barnabus and Saul for the work to which I have called them'" (Acts 13:2). These men left Antioch to preach and teach in many cities throughout Asia, before returning. Through the work of Paul and Barnabus, the church at Antioch helped other churches.

Pastors and churches often need the help of other churches. Being part of a larger fellowship of many churches helps them work effectively.

The third reason many churches share together is because they have the *same work to do* and can do it better together than alone. The mission of believers in local churches is worldwide. An individual church usually doesn't have the money necessary to send missions workers to other countries. Few churches can support a camping program for Christians, but the group churches which make up your District do just that. They also train people to be better teachers and do many other important tasks.

YOUR CHURCH SHARES ITS FAITH, INTERESTS AND WORK WITH OTHER BAPTIST CHURCHES.

Districts plan many events such as retreats, concerts and campouts, so Christians from many churches can have fellowship together. This is very valuable because it helps people understand each other and see the strength of the church.

The Baptist General Conference itself (your District is one of sixteen that make up the BGC) performs jobs that even the Districts find too large. The world missions program supports missions on several continents, starting new churches. The objective of the home missions board is to start and strengthen churches all across North America.

The Conference educational centers at Bethel College and Seminary train people to serve as Christians in all kinds of work. This includes working as pastors, Christian education instructors and mission workers. The Christian education board publishes and provides books to inspire believers and help them work well for God.

These large responsibilities could not easily be carried out by individual churches or even small groups of churches. That is why the churches that make up the BGC have joined together in fellowship. Together they share the great work which the Lord has given the church to do.

An Even Greater Fellowship

There are many groups who aren't Baptists with which Baptist churches join in fellowship. These churches have most of the basic beliefs that Baptists share and which are found in this book. We do not join in fellowship with churches that oppose our basic beliefs.

There are several reasons that Baptists have fellowship with other kinds of churches. First, the New Testament makes it clear that all Christians are part of one, eternal church. Jesus prayed to the Father that this would happen. "I pray also for those who will believe in me through their message, that all of them may be one, Father, just as you are in me and I am in you...I have given them the glory that you gave me, *that they may be one* as we are one..." (John 17:20-22). Paul confirmed that this had happened when he said "there is one body," and believers want to show that they believe this is so.

We can have fellowship with any church or believer who lives under the authority of the Bible and loves Jesus as Lord. Just as in a family, there is room for differing ideas and opinions. As long as we agree on basic things.

A second reason churches should fellowship together is because a united "voice" is sometimes heard more clearly than separate voices. In some things, leaders in our states, country and in other countries will listen to our united voice more quickly than to individuals. This influence can make big projects for Christ possible. Some examples are feeding starving people, drilling wells, teaching people how to raise crops, how to read and to write.

Another reason for a larger fellowship is to protect Christians' religious freedom. Groups of churches join with each other to hire people who will keep track of new laws and legal decisions made in the U.S. government that will affect Christian freedom. Sometimes these people who work with the government are able to help people in other parts of the world. People who are being mistreated because of their beliefs or have had their possessions taken from them.

CHRISTIAN FELLOWSHIP EXTENDS BEYOND YOUR CHURCH. YOU CAN HAVE FELLOWSHIP WITH ANYONE WHO IS UNDER THE AUTHORITY OF CHRIST.

Things to Do

1. If you wanted a friend to come to your Sunday school class or youth group, how would you describe the group to him or her? What would you tell your friend about your Christian friends that would make him or her want to know them?

2. What did Jesus pray for all Christians in every generation (see John 17:20-21)?

3. How many reasons can you find in this chapter for believers worshiping in local churches?

4. Why do Baptist churches have fellowship with other churches who believe basically as they do?

a.

b.

c.

11 Worship: Our Response to a Holy God

"Are you getting up, Jeff?" Dad called from outside the tent.

Jeff lay in his sleeping bag, listening to his parents unpacking breakfast stuff from the trunk of the car. They had arrived and set up two nights earlier. He wasn't interested in going to church that morning. He wanted to play sick and then explore the campground when they left. But he knew they wouldn't leave without him.

"I'm coming," he replied reluctantly.

"Better hurry," his mother answered. "Breakfast will be ready in five minutes and church begins in half an hour."

"I said I'm coming," Jeff repeated. He crawled out of the sleeping bag and quickly pulled on his clothes. The morning air was crisp.

Breakfast was ready by the time he fumbled his way out of the tent, using both hands in a desperate attempt to matt down his hair.

"You'd better change your shirt after we eat," his mother said. Jeff poured milk on his cereal and sat down.

"Do I have to go to church this morning?" he asked. "Why can't I stay here?"

"We are staying here," Jeff's dad replied. "There's an open air sanctuary down by the road. The view is tremendous."

"We're going there?" Jeff asked. They usually visited small town churches while on vacation.

"Yes," his mother answered. "One of the local pastors comes to the campground on Sunday mornings."

"Then I don't have to change my shirt?"

"You don't have to, but you should look nice," his dad replied. "The sign at the office said 'Come as you are.' You may enjoy it."

Jeff shrugged and dug into his cereal.

He was surprised when he saw the open air sanctuary. It was majestic. It was built on a hillside with split log benches descending towards a rough pine altar. The trees opened up behind the altar, framing the snowcapped peaks. To the right, the morning sun was spearing through the tops of the pines. The sky was a deep blue, spotted with thick, white clouds.

Jeff and his parents sat in the third row. The pastor had placed hymnals on each of the benches and was greeting people as they arrived. The service soon began.

Jeff felt differently than he usually felt in church. The sky, the stately trees and the mountains made him feel God's presence in an entirely new way. It was as if Jesus were standing at the back of the sanctuary. He was more alert in church than he had been for a long time. He knew God was there.

They sang about God's work as the Creator and Jeff really understood the words. The pastor spoke about the way God reveals Himself to man through nature and through His Son. When the service was over, Jeff didn't want to leave. God was so real to him, so alive, that he wanted to keep singing. He felt that he really meant it when he prayed and sang that morning. And it seemed that God had revealed something new about

Himself.

Jeff's experience is one that all Christian's desire. Rather than singing and doing things mechanically as he usually did in church, Jeff truly worshiped God that morning. It gave him a new understanding and delight in God's presence. That is what worship is—a person's response to God revealing Himself. It brings a new understanding and delight in God's presence. And it pleases God.

Worship involves both us and God. We both give and receive when we worship. We give praise, reverence and thanks to God, telling Him our sins and asking for His forgiveness. We receive understanding, instruction and the joy of being in His presence.

WORSHIP IS THE BELIEVER'S RESPONSE TO WHO GOD IS AND WHAT HE DOES.

The New Testament gives more than one pattern or way of worship that we can follow. The important thing is that a church worships in ways that are guided by God.

The New Testament tells us many things about true worship. Four important ideas are that worship is spiritual, direct, understandable and sincere.

Worship Is Spiritual

Many people don't enjoy times of worship because they do it for the wrong reasons. They pray, sing, read the Bible or hear the sermon because they feel that they "should" rather than really than wanting to. In actuality, they are not worshiping at all. Jesus told a woman from Samaria what true worship is like. He said, "Yet a time is coming and has now come when the true worshipers will worship the Father in spirit and truth, for they are the kind of worshipers the Father seeks. God is spirit, and his worshipers must *worship in spirit and in truth*" (John 4:23,24).

This requires some explanation. First, what is worshiping in spirit? When a person becomes a Christian, he or she receives the Holy Spirit into his or her soul. Jesus said, "I will ask the Father, and He will give you another Counselor to be with you forever—the Spirit of Truth...you know him, for he lives with you and will be in you" (John 14:16,17). God's Spirit lives within the Christian and helps him to learn about Christ and to live like Him. To worship in spirit, then, means in part that we cooperate and follow the direction of the Holy Spirit. Especially as He helps us center our attention on God. *As we pray and sing with the help of God's Spirit, we are responding to God rather than thinking about ourselves. We respond to who He is, to what He's done, to what He's doing.* This response comes from within us, with the help of God's Spirit. It doesn't depend on any special place, atmosphere or ritual.

Because it is spiritual, the most important part of worship is attitude. An attitude of desiring to be with God and to praise and please Him will honor God. If God is truly important to a Christian, then he or she will approach Him with respect and awe. Churches often choose appropriate songs and a beginning prayer to help worshipers focus their attention on God.

WORSHIP IS SPIRITUAL. IT IS GUIDED BY GOD'S SPIRIT.

Worship Is Direct

Have you ever asked somebody to give a message to a really close friend? What often happens is that your friend gets a slightly different message than you originally gave and thinks you said something that you really didn't. It's much easier to talk directly with your friend. You know you'll be understood.

Worship is direct. It is direct communication between you and God, made possible by God's Spirit. Nobody interprets or misinterprets your conversation. Nobody puts words in your mouth.

People who lead in a worship service must be able to help others experience this direct communication with God. For example, when the pastor prays, each person should quietly pray along with him, speaking directly to God.

When you pray, say "thank you" to God for what He has done. God wants you to ask Him directly for things you need. He wants you to ask Him for help for other people. For example, you might pray for missionaries and people who are traveling or sick. God also wants you to pray for the needs of city, state and national government leaders.

Music also helps us come directly to God. In Psalm 147:1, David sang the following words: "How good it is to sing praises *to our God,* how pleasant and fitting to praise him!" Psalm 149 and 150 are about praising God with songs and musical instruments. Some of the instruments were the tambourine, harp, trumpet, strings, flute and cymbals. The kind of instrument is not that important. What is important is that our worship through music helps us focus on God and come directly to him, rather than focus on ourselves.

WORSHIP IS DIRECT COMMUNICATION BETWEEN YOU AND GOD.

Worship Is Understandable

Have you ever watched part of a television program that was in another language? You may be able to guess part of what is going on from what the people do, but if you don't know the language most of it doesn't make sense.

Some people think worship is like that. Someone else does things which are supposed to be important, while other people watch and don't really know what's going on. Two things are wrong with this. First, worship is something every Christian should do. There aren't performers and viewers as in a concert. Everyone is a performer. The second thing wrong is that worship isn't a secret that only a few people can know. It is meant to be understood by everyone.

Remember that Jesus said to the woman from Samaria that God's worshipers "must worship in spirit and in truth"? Worship in truth is centering our attention on spiritual truth that we receive through the Scriptures. In worship, therefore, Baptists place emphasis on the Bible. They believe that it is the inspired Word of God and it was written to point people toward the living Son of God,

Jesus Christ. The Bible helps us understand who God is, what He has done and how we can know Him.

Reading the Bible is an important part of worship. It's not included in a worship service just to take up time. Reading or listening to the Bible being read during worship helps us understand God and learn about Him. Those who read out loud should speak clearly, emphasizing meaningful words and phrases. Those who listen should pay attention by reading along or trying to learn what the Scripture says.

The pastor's message is another part of worship that helps believers understand God better. The pastor takes this responsibility very seriously by studying the Bible and praying sincerely. The worshipers need to listen carefully to what he says and compare it with their own growing knowledge of the Bible.

WORSHIP MUST INVOLVE OUR UNDERSTANDING.

Worship Is Sincere

In ancient times, pottery dealers sold a very high quality porcelain which was highly prized and expensive. The porcelain was very fragile and often it cracked when hardened in the fire. Dishonest dealers filled the cracks with a white wax that matched the porcelain. It couldn't be detected unless the object was held up to the light. Then the wax would clearly show up as a dark seam. Honest dealers marked their pottery with the words *sine cera,* which means without wax. The word sincere comes from this original Latin term.

Sincere worship is part of worshiping in truth. There is nothing fake about it and we can't fake out God. Being honest with God means not faking happiness or sadness before God. It means not pretending that we're better than we really are. Jesus had some very harsh words for religious leaders in His time who tried to fool God. "You hypocrites!" He said, "Isaiah was right when he prophesied about you:

'These people honor me with their lips, but their hearts are far from me. They worship me in vain; their teachings are but rules taught by men!'" (Matthew 15:7-9).

Jesus obviously knew that people could have an untrue worship.

Sincere worship happens when the believer is listening to God and waiting to hear His message. Whispering, scuffling and not paying attention tell God that we are not very interested. This is especially true during prayer. A sincere worshiper is open to hear God's message in every part of the worship service.

WORSHIP IS SINCERE. THE BELIEVER IS LISTENING TO GOD.

Our worship is our response to God and we respond in many ways. We praise Him, sing, pray, learn from the Bible and from the pastor's message. True worship will cause us to respond to what we learn from God. In the quiet moments at the end of a service we may ask God to change the things in our life which we've learned are displeasing to Him. We may do this quietly on our own, or publicly, going to the front of the church. If we are obedient to God, He will help us to become more like Christ.

Worship is a person's response to who God is and what He does. It brings us a new delight and understanding of Him. It also gives glory to God. Bible reading, music, praise and prayer are all good ways to worship. But worship must be spiritual, direct, understandable and sincere if it is to please God and have an effect on the way we live. The most important part of worship is the believer's attitude. An attitude of desiring to be with God, to please Him and praise him, will honor God. Jesus desires the best a Christian has to offer, and this includes his or her attitude as he or she worships.

Things to Do

1. How would you tell a friend what "worship" is?

2. How do you know that God is looking for people that want to worship Him (John 14:16-17)

3. List four important ideas about the kind of worship that pleases God.

4. Contrast wrong ways to worship God with right ways that please Him.

12 God + Ideas
     + People
     = History

Karen stared out the window as the train began to move. Her mother waved to her from the platform. Even as Karen waved back she was aware that she probably wouldn't see her mom again for at least a year, if not more. She could hardly believe that she was leaving.

Karen's parents were divorced. She was leaving the small midwestern town where she grew up and going to live with her father in a city of several million people. She didn't know what it would be like there and she was a little afraid. She already missed her mom and her friends.

The train turned to the left as it pulled away from the station. She could no longer see her mom or even the platform. It was dark outside. As she watched the grain elevators and railroad crossings slip past the window, it seemed that she was leaving everything she'd ever known. Her mother, friends at school, church, the neighborhood she knew so well, even her cat. She knew that somehow her life would be completely different, and the people and things she had known so well would be replaced by new people and new things. But she didn't want that to happen!

The train continued onward for hours, stopping occasionally. The lights of the small towns looked greenish and unreal through the tinted glass. When they crossed a wide, black river it suddenly hit her that from that moment onward her past would be gone. In fact, she might never see her mom, friends and home town again. She decided that she would remember everything. She would make a strong effort to remember every person, every place, every detail, so that her first home would always be with her—in her mind. Maybe she would even write it down to help her remember.

Writing down important events of the past is called history, and Karen's experience shows us the importance of history. Knowing what has happened in the past helps us know who we are now, so we can face the future with confidence. This is also true in the history of the church. Churches today need to know about their roots in the past, how they got started and how they have come to be what they are today.

Here is a brief description of the way the church has grown and changed throughout history, showing where Baptists fit in.

Cruel Treatment

The first Christians met in their homes. When people joined the groups, these groups moved into larger buildings. As more people became Christians, non-Christians began to resent and abuse them. For the first three hundred years Christians were treated cruelly by both the Jews and the Romans. Both wanted to destroy them. The Roman emperors Nero and Diocletian enjoyed hurting Christians They wanted to destroy the religion. Christians were beaten, whipped, murdered and driven out of their cities. But this mistreatment, as cruel as it was, brought change and growth. The Christian church was planted in more and more countries until the Roman Empire was changed into a "somewhat" Christian country.

The Dark Ages

In 313 A.D. the Roman emperor Constantine made Christianity the official religion of Rome. He combined the church and the empire.

Unfortunately, this led to many evils. For example, it was actually possible to pay someone to buy an important job in the church. Church leaders became politically powerful and were often corrupt. This situation created the period in history often called The Dark Ages.

Nearly everyone in Europe belonged to the church then, but few people took their religion seriously. Many wrong ideas became part of church operations during this time. Some examples are prayers for dead people, worship of Mary, worship of saints and images and the selling of fake forgiveness for sin. The church became very wealthy and powerful during this period of over a thousand years, but it gradually lost its spiritual influence. Churches thought that their history and their own decisions were more important than the teachings of the Bible.

The Reformation

Have you ever worked with clay? If you have, then you've probably made something, didn't like it, and then reshaped the clay to make something else. You *reformed* the shape of the clay.

In the 1500s, a period of history began which is called The Reformation. It got that name because the church was in many ways reformed by people who saw the wickedness which existed in the church. One well known man of that time was Martin Luther. He protested against much of what was being taught in churches of his time.

Luther tried to get the church to return to using the Bible as its guide. The church leaders that agreed with him started new churches which were no longer under the leadership of the church in Rome. Many churches in America today began as a result of Luther and other leaders who worked to purify the church.

Luther wasn't the first man who tried to clean the wickedness and ungodliness out of the church. Others before him started the work which he expanded. One was Arnold of Brescia, a city in northern Italy. A priest there, he tried to change things by reporting the sins of church leaders. He insisted that the church should be spiritual and its members born again. He also taught that the church and government should operate separately. Because of what he taught, he was hanged in Rome in 1155.

Peter Waldo, a wealthy merchant from Lyons, France, became another reformer. He felt that God had asked him to live in poverty. A group of disciples formed, following his habits of unselfishness and daily preaching salvation through Christ. They believed 1) the Bible, rather than the Pope, should be obeyed; 2) the teachings of purgatory and confession should be given up because they are not in the Bible; 3) selling of forgiveness of sins was wrong; and 4) all church members should have the right to preach. Peter Waldo lived in the late 1100s.

John Wycliffe, an English scholar, was another reformer. He translated the Bible into English so that not only church leaders could read it. He lived in the late 1300s.

Wycliffe's ideas were taught in Europe by John Huss of Bohemia. He was a priest who preached against the sins of the church leaders and insisted that anyone should be able to read the Bible for himself. The Pope said "No" to that in 1409. Huss was considered guilty of rebellion against the Pope and burned at the stake in July 1415. He died preaching from the Bible and singing a hymn.

These were some of the important reformers before The Reformation, and they prepared the way for men like Luther, Calvin and Zwingli.

DURING THE REFORMATION, MANY CHURCHES RETURNED TO USING THE BIBLE AS THEIR SPIRITUAL AUTHORITY.

Anabaptists

It was during this time of change in the church that a group called the Anabaptists began to appear. The name means "rebaptizers" and was a nickname given to the group by people who mocked them. They baptized again those who had been sprinkled as babies or children, because they did not believe that sprinkling was taught in the New Testament. They believed that the New Testament shows that baptism always comes after becoming a Christian, not before, and it is to be done only by immersion.

They also believed that the Bible is the final authority for the church. They thought that the church and the government should be kept separate and that only born again believers should become church members. They first organized as a group in Switzerland. They were severely mistreated and abused, because even the great leaders of the Reformation believed that baptism by sprinkling was all right.

THE ANABAPTISTS WERE ONE OF THE FORERUNNERS OF OUR PRESENT BAPTIST CHURCHES.

An outstanding Anabaptist leader was Balthaser Hubmaier, a Roman

Catholic priest who lived in Austria from 1480 to 1528. He believed that faith in Jesus must come before baptism and that religion was a person's own choice. It shouldn't be forced on anyone. He also believed that the Bible alone ought to be the guide for living the Christian life. He was burned at the stake for what he taught and his wife was drowned in the Danube River. That was the fate of many Anabaptists during this period.

The first actual Baptist church was founded under the leadership of John Smyth of England. He and his followers were forced to leave the country, so they went to Amsterdam, Holland. They formed a Baptist church there in about 1608. Around 1610 part of this group returned to England, where Baptist churches began to spread. They were mistreated for their faith until 1689, when it became legal in England to follow any religion one chooses.

Baptists In the United States

Many early American settlers came from England, where they had been mistreated and abused because of their religious beliefs. One of these was Roger Williams, pastor in Plymouth County, Massachusetts. He began to believe that the government shouldn't interfere with the church. Many early colonists disagreed. They had fled England and Europe to have religious freedom for themselves. However, when they got to America they didn't want anyone who disagreed with their beliefs to have religious freedom. So they drove Roger Williams out of their colony.

In the middle of the winter of January, 1636, Williams struggled through the wilderness. Indians that he had helped previously, saved his life. In Providence, Rhode Island, in 1638, he led in starting a colony that allowed religious freedom for everyone. In 1639 he accepted Baptist views and was baptized by immersion. Ten other people were then baptized and they began the First Baptist Church of Providence, which is still active today.

This was only the beginning of religous freedom in America. Much bloodshed and abuse was endured in most of the 13 colonies so that we might have the freedom we enjoy today. Baptists were hunted and molested, whipped, imprisoned, fined and publicly disgraced in every imaginable way. Yet with all of this abuse, by 1740 there were already 47 Baptist churches.

RELIGIOUS LIBERTY IS AN IMPORTANT BAPTIST BELIEF.

Influence and Growth

Baptists have made some outstanding contributions to the United States and the world. For example, the American Bill of Rights (which allows many freedoms) came primarily from the democratic beliefs and actions of Baptist in Virginia. The first modern missionary was William Carey, a Baptist from England. The first American foreign missionary was also a Baptist: Adoniram Judson. Charles Spurgeon, one of the greatest preachers in history, was a Baptist. And the first Sunday school in America was started at First Baptist Church of Philadelphia in 1815.

In 1739 an exceptional English preacher named George Whitefield came and spoke in America. His preaching and that of other ministers caused many people to come to Christ. Baptist churches grew very quickly as a result.

By 1792 there were 471 Baptist churches with 35,000 members in the U.S. In 1800 there were 10,000. By 1900 there were over 4,000,000 and in 1945 14,000,000. By the mid-1980s there were more than 35,000,000 Baptists in North America.

BAPTISTS HAVE MADE OUTSTANDING CONTRIBUTIONS IN THE WORLD.

The Baptist General Conference

The Baptist General Conference is a name that describes a group of more than 800 churches which are joined to tell the world about salvation through Jesus Christ. It began among Swedish immigrants. Many of these immigrants left Sweden because they were treated harshly for their Baptist beliefs. In Galesburg, Illinois, a man named Gustaf Palmquist was baptized by immersion and made pastor of a church. Seven weeks later, on August 13, 1852, he baptized three people in nearby Rock Island, Illinois. Together they began a new church there, the First Swedish Baptist church in America. This was the first church of the Baptist General Conference. Other churches soon started in Iowa, Maine, New York City and towns in Illinois.

The beginnings of the Baptist General Conference were slow. By 1864 there were only eleven churches, with a total of 360 members. By 1952, 100 years after the first church was founded, there were slightly less than 50,000 members of the BGC (Baptist General Conference). In 1984 there were over 135,000 in approximately 800 churches.

God has been at work in our fellowship of churches. In 1944 a major change took place in the BGC. Up to that time the BGC had worked through other church organizations to send out mission workers. But in 1944 the Conference decided to train and send out its own missionaries. That change sparked growth in many other parts of our work, as the BGC carried forth its own mission for Christ.

While the Baptist General Conference claims August 13, 1852 as the day it began, its beliefs are based on the importance of the Bible and necessity of personal faith in Christ. These ideas trace back to the first Christians in Jerusalem. They were ideas that were nearly crushed under Roman domination and the Dark Ages. But they plainly emerged again in the Reformation. From Anabaptists of the Reformation came the first Baptist churches in England. And from England came the first Baptists in America. In other countries these ideas also took hold.

As Swedish immigrants who wanted freedom to worship as Baptists came to America, the beginning of our fellowship of churches took place. We are still growing, and thankful for God's protection of His truth and His People, and our place among His people as the Baptist General Conference.

THE BAPTIST GENERAL CONFERENCE IS OUR GROUP OF CHURCHES THAT ARE JOINED TO TELL THE WORLD ABOUT SALVATION THROUGH JESUS CHRIST.

Things to Do

1. Complete this sentence: I am grateful for my Baptist heritage because . . .

2. Why mistakes did the Roman emperor Constantine make when he declared Christianity to be the official religion of Rome in 313 A.D.

3. What was wrong with the church during the Dark Ages?

4. Who were the forerunners of our present Baptist churches?

5. What are some things you enjoy today which Baptists of the past made possible?

13 Similar, Yet Different

Keith Harding was different from the other counselors at camp that summer. Randy noticed it first and immediately told Dennis, Steve and two other boys.

Randy and Dennis were washing up for dinner. A wasp was buzzing against the window screen and several faucets were steadily dripping. "Did you hear music this morning?" Randy asked.

"Yeah, it sounded like a flute or something," Dennis replied. "It was weird."

"It was the counselor, Keith," Randy said. "I heard him playing it last night, right after we went to bed."

"My grandmother likes that kind of music," Dennis scowled.

They went outside and started towards the main lodge. "There he is," Randy pointed. "Come on."

They caught up with Keith on the porch.

"Do you really play a flute?" Randy asked.

Keith nodded, opening the door for the boys.

"Why do you play old fashioned stuff?" Dennis inquired.

"I like all kinds of music," Keith answered. "I'm studying music in college. As for preferring classical to other kinds of music, I guess it just makes me feel better inside than the others do. That's why I like to play it."

"Don't you listen to rock and roll?" Randy asked.

"Yes, sometimes," Keith nodded. They found an open table and sat down together.

"But you like classical stuff more?" Dennis asked.

"Yes, most of the time," Keith agreed.

"Not me," Dennis objected, "rock and roll is the greatest."

Randy hesitated for a moment, and then said, "Classical stuff is okay," "but I'm not sure what I like best. I do like to hear you play the flute at night. It sounds neat."

"Yeah, and we both think you're the best counselor here this year," Dennis added.

"Thank you," Keith nodded.

"We don't mind that you're different," Randy added.

People are different from each other

in many ways. Some like different music than you do, different clothes or different churches. Like people, churches have many differences. Each church has several ideas that its members agree to.

In the churches of the Baptist General Conference, members agree to eight basic ideas which guide what they do and how they live. You may already know what some of these ideas are; they have been mentioned in the chapters of this book. These eight ideas make Baptists distinct from other churches.

8 Basic Baptist Beliefs

1) *The New Testament is the only authority for faith and actions.* Baptists believe that the entire Bible was written by God through men, but it is the New Testament that gives us the authority for the ways we live and what we believe. No other official statements in the church have the power to be our complete guide. We look for answers and principles in the New Testament before looking anywhere else.

2) *God allows every person to come directly to Himself through Jesus Christ.* According to the New Testament, everyone who believes and follows Jesus Christ is a priest to God. No other person or powerful group of people can interfere with another person's relationship to God. This puts every person on equal

footing before God.

3) *The church and the government are completely separate, neither making rules for the other to follow.* The government shouldn't interfere with the spiritual functions of churches (church services, meetings, church elections, etc). It can neither make one religion official for the whole country nor deny people the right to worship as they please. Churches can speak out if the government violates biblical or moral principles.

4) *Our church has a simple, democratic form of government.* Each member in a Baptist church has as much authority as every other member, including the pastor. Each church makes it own decisions—no other group of people tell a church what it must do. Many Baptist churches work together in a large group such as our Baptist General Conference. This group starts churches, sends missionaries into the mission fields, publishes books and does other things that single or small groups of churches cannot do.

5) *Baptism is for believers only and only by immersion.* To be baptized, you must be old enough to understand what it means to become a Christian and have accepted Jesus Christ as your Lord and Savior. The New Testament shows that

baptism can only be done by dipping someone completely under water. This shows that we are like Jesus in His death, burial and resurrection. Christians should be baptized in obedience to Christ, publicly showing people in the church that they have received new life. Baptism will not make you a Christian. It is a response to having already become one.

6) *Only Christians can become members of Baptist churches.* Anyone desiring to join a Baptist church should be able to show real evidences of his faith in Christ. He or she may be asked to tell how and when he began to trust in Christ and how his life has changed since then.

7) *Jesus is the supreme Head of the church.* Everything that is done in the church should be under the control of Jesus Christ. No group of people in the church can take control. All are under Christ's authority. Each individual needs to be obedient to Christ and honest, kind, humble and loving with other people.

8) *The church's job is to tell everyone in the world about Jesus, helping them to become Christians.* Jesus commanded every Christian to tell other people about His life, death, burial and resurrection. Christians are then to encourage those people as they confess their sins and receive Him as Lord and Savior. Christ said all nations must hear about Him. The

Baptist General Conference is a group of churches organized together to help fulfill this command around the world. Nonetheless, each Christian is responsible to share his or her faith with non-Christians around him.

These eight ideas are basic Baptist beliefs. They distinguish us from other churches, though many other churches may share some of these beliefs. They are derived from the teachings of the New Testament and give direction to the way Baptist churches function. While we believe these are true guidelines for the church, we strongly support the freedom of others to disagree.

Before You Turn the Page...

Now you have some ideas about who Baptists are, what they are like and what they believe. Are these your ideas? Do you believe them yourself? Maybe you aren't even sure if you are a Christian. It is important to be sure. If you want to be sure you are a Christian, then review the section in chapter four entitled "Spiritual Life." Study the Scriptures listed in that passage and ask God to help you understand them. Your parents, or others in your family, may be Christians and you can talk with them about your desire to know Jesus. Your pastor will also be happy to talk with you about faith in

Christ.

If you are a Christian and want to be baptized, then read chapter five again to become familiar with the main ideas. Then talk to your parents, pastor, or one of the leaders in your church.

If you have questions about anything you've read in this book, don't feel afraid to ask them. Your parents and church leaders can help you understand anything which you find puzzling or unclear.

This book was written to help you "...live a life worthy of the Lord and... please him in every way: bearing fruit in every good work, growing in the knowledge of God..." (Colossians 1:10). We pray that it will help you as you grow into His likeness.

Things to Do

1. There are eight ideas which make Baptist churches distinct from all other churches. Cross out the wrong word or words in each sentence and replace it with the right word or words.
a. The Old Testament is the only authority for faith and actions.
b. God allows special people to come directly to Himself through Jesus Christ.
c. The church and the government are completely joined, either making rules for the other to follow.

d. Our church is a simple, autocratic form of government.

e. Baptism is for believers only and only by sprinkling.

f. Only Christians can become members of Baptist unions.

g. The pastor is the supreme Head of the church.

h. The church's job is to tell everyone in America about Jesus, helping them to become church members.

2. Think back over the ideas you studied in this book. Which have meant the most to you and why?

Dictionary

Baptism
The lowering of a believer under water, as a picture of Jesus' death and resurrection. Baptism also shows the believer's new life in Christ and the end of his/her own control of life.

Forgiveness
To lovingly pardon rather than to punish. God's pardon of someone who admits his/her sins and asks Jesus to save him/her.

Holy
Perfect. Separate from sin. God is holy and able to make those who believe in His Son free from sin, holy.

Immerse
To dip or submerge under water. The New Testament shows that baptism should be done by immersion.

Local Church
A group of Christians who live in one area and join together under the leadership of Christ. They worship God together and help each other. They also work together to share their faith, love, time and possessions with other people.

The Lord's Supper
Believers eating and drinking together to remember Christ's death, in a ceremony using bread as a picture of Christ's body and grape juice as a picture of His shed blood. Often called communion.

Ordinance
A law or commandment. Jesus commanded His followers to be baptized and to observe the Lord's Supper. Both are "ordinances" in the Baptist church.

Priest
A person who has direct access to God through Jesus Christ. His or her task is to help other people meet and know God.

Repentance
Changing your mind about sin. Understanding the seriousness of sin, and turning away from it to God for forgiveness.

Resurrection
Being made alive again after being dead. Jesus was resurrected on Easter morning.

Righteousness
Being made right and acting rightly before God and people. Becoming like Jesus.

Salvation

Being rescued from sin and its results. Being brought to a right relationship with God, through faith in Jesus Christ. Our experience of forgiveness.

Sin

Disobedience to God. Rebellion against God—especially against the teachings of the New Testament.

Steward

One who manages another's property. Since God owns everything, a Christian must manage well what God has entrusted to him or her. All believers should be good managers of their time, special abilities and possessions.

Worship

To honor God. To give praise, thanks and requests to God. Worship may be silent, spoken or with music.

Some Events in Baptist History

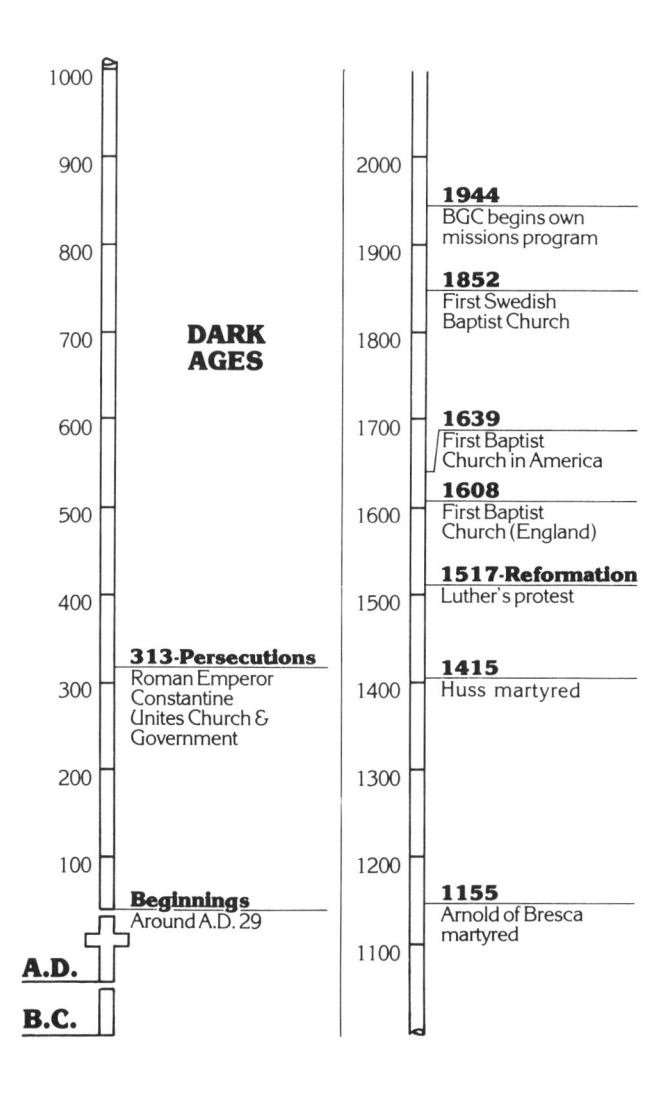

Beginnings — Around A.D. 29

313 - Persecutions
Roman Emperor Constantine Unites Church & Government

DARK AGES

1155
Arnold of Brescia martyred

1415
Huss martyred

1517 - Reformation
Luther's protest

1608
First Baptist Church (England)

1639
First Baptist Church in America

1852
First Swedish Baptist Church

1944
BGC begins own missions program